ELAHEH ROSTAMI-POVEY

Afghan women

Identity and invasion

Zed Books
LONDON | NEW YORK

Afghan women: identity and invasion was first published in 2007 by Zed Books Ltd, 7 Cynthia Street, London N1 9JF, UK and Room 400, 175 Fifth Avenue, New York, NY 10010, USA

www.zedbooks.co.uk

Cover designed by Andrew Corbett
Set in Arnhem and Futura Bold by Ewan Smith, London
Index: ed.emery@thefreeuniversity.net
Printed and bound in Malta by Gutenberg Press

Distributed in the USA exclusively by Palgrave Macmillan, a division of St Martin's Press, LLC, 175 Fifth Avenue, New York, NY 10010.

A catalogue record for this book is available from the British Library.
Library of Congress cataloging in publication data are available.

ISBN 978 1 84277 855 5 hb
ISBN 978 1 84277 856 2 pb

Contents

Acknowledgements | vii Glossary | ix
Acronyms | x Preface | xi Map | xii

1 Introduction 1

Gender, ethnicity, agency and identity | 3
A short history | 9 The structure of the book | 13

2 Resistance and struggle under the Taliban 16

Communal identity and gender relations | 17
The civil war and the Taliban period | 19
The experiences of Afghan women under the Taliban | 26 Women's survival strategies | 28

3 Under invasion 40

International security forces | 47 The UN and international NGOs | 50 The state, foreign private companies and the warlords | 53 The opium economy | 55 Women and reconstruction | 59
Education | 65 Returned refugees | 67 Pornography and Bollywood | 70 Is Afghanistan better now? | 74

4 Exile and identity 80

Migration to Iran and Pakistan | 80 Migration to the USA and the UK | 89 Diasporic consciousness in Iran and Pakistan | 94 Exile, history and Afghan futures | 98
Changing gender relations in the context of Islamic culture | 102 Diasporic consciousness: the impact of 9/11 and 7/7 on Afghan women | 111 Conclusion | 126

5 Challenging domination 129

The imperial agenda | 137

Bibliography | 143
Index | 153

I dedicate this book to my children and grandchildren, Tara, Farhad, Lily, Lara, Amy, Behnam and Behrang for their love and support

Acknowledgements

I have worked on this book since 2002 and am indebted to numerous people and institutions, in particular my partner, John Rose, for reading the entire manuscript and for his detailed and insightful suggestions and critical care that enriched my thinking. I owe much to Sanam Rostami, Siamak Aboutaleb and Roya Rostami for translating 200 interviews and sorting out hundreds of photographs with impeccable professionalism, enabling me to present to you the voices of Afghan women. My heartfelt thanks go to my family, Daryoush, Nahid, Ahmad, Jane, Sadaf and Maryam, for their encouragement and love which kept me going.

I presented my ideas at the Development Studies Association, Women and Development Study Group, at York University and the London Middle East Institute at the School of Oriental and African Studies and greatly benefited from stimulating and challenging discussions which broadened my thinking. I am, in particular, indebted to the intellectual support of Haleh Afshar and Ziba Mir-Hosseini. Haleh Afshar, Chris Rundle, Joan Smith, Mehri Honarbin-Holliday and Alessandro Monsutti have read the earlier versions and parts of this book and made invaluable suggestions and corrections. Ellen McKinlay, my editor at Zed Books, was a tremendous intellectual support; her curiosity, criticism, expertise and good-will made it possible for me to write this book.

My debt to friends and colleagues is immeasurable. Without them my contribution to this project would have been limited: Mahbobeh Abbasgholizadeh, Orzala Ashraf, Nayereh Toohidi, Zohra Yusuf Daoud, Shahbibi Shah, Suhaila Ismat, Martin Lau, Nasira Moheb, Nahid Ashrafi,

Setareh Saedi, Afsaneh Ashrafi, Massoumeh Farman-Farmaian, Homa Hoodfar, Zohreh Hosseini, Marzia Adil, Kolsom Bazi, Sara Kamal, Saeed Khan, Shafi Mohammed, Meena Baktash, Nushin Arabzadeh, Eliza Hilton, Angela Schlenkhoff, Atikah Chowdhury and Michelle Delgado. Many of these friends and colleagues made it possible for me to interview women and men in Afghanistan, Iran, Pakistan, the UK and USA. UNHCR and UNICEF in Tehran, Mashhad, Peshawar and Karachi, Sherkatgah, the Afghan Women's Network, the Afghan Women Council, Humanitarian Assistance for Women and Children of Afghanistan, the Revolutionary Association of Women of Afghanistan and the BBC World Service Trust were also of tremendous help. Finally, my special thanks go to the Economic Social Research Council (ESRC UK) for funding this project in 2004–05.

Glossary

Al-Amr bi-al-mar.ruf wa-al-nahy an almunkar – the promotion of virtue and prevention of vice

burqa or *chaddari* – loose garment completely covering a woman's body and face

Loya Jirga – Grand Assembly

madrassa – religious school

mahram – women to be accompanied by their husbands or blood male relatives

Mujaheddin – fighters in holy wars

Pashtunwali – the customary law of the Pashtuns

Shari'a – Islamic law

Acronyms

AIHRC	Afghanistan Independent Human Rights Commission
AREU	Afghanistan Research and Evaluation Unit
AWC	Afghan Women Council
AWN	Afghan Women Network
CIA	Central Intelligence Agency
DFID	Department for International Development
HAWCA	Humanitarian Assistance for the Women and Children of Afghanistan
IMF	International Monetary Fund
INGOTC	Iranian NGO Training Centre
ISAF	International Security Assistance Force
MSF	Médecins Sans Frontières
NATO	North Atlantic Treaty Organization
NGO	non-governmental organization
NSS	National Security Strategy
PDPA	People's Democratic Party of Afghanistan
PRT	Provincial Reconstruction Team
RAWA	Revolutionary Association of the Women of Afghanistan
TNCs	transnational corporations
UNDP	United Nations Development Programme
UNHCR	United Nations High Commissioner for Refugees
UNICEF	United Nations Children's Fund
UNODC	United Nations Office on Drugs and Crime
UNSC	United Nations Security Council
WTO	World Trade Organization

Preface

This book is intended to counter the often inaccurate and misleading impressions put about by the media and politicians in the West when they talk about Afghanistan and Afghan women in particular. It is a contribution to the global peace movement and the struggle of millions of people against the continuation of the wars and conflicts orchestrated by George W. Bush, Tony Blair and Condoleezza Rice. It is also a challenge to western feminists who do not try to understand women in Muslim majority societies and cultures, and who today do not take a stand against the misogynistic culture of neo-liberalism and neo-conservatism that promotes western superiority and the imperial strategy of 'saving Afghan and Muslim women'. This passive stance has allowed their ideas to be hijacked by the particularly aggressive new imperialism of the twentieth-first-century, which has successfully manipulated their ideas for its own economic and political power-seeking. I include in this discussion the current reactivation of Islamophobia, fear of Islam: Afghan women in the West alongside other practising Muslim women have been the victims of this contemporary racist discourse. The future of women's rights in Afghanistan does not just depend on challenging local male domination, but also on challenging imperial domination.

Map of Afghanistan

1 | Introduction

> 'When the civil war came to Afghanistan the little but significant that was achieved by women came to a standstill. War steals the very breath that life offers, and Afghanistan stopped breathing.' Zohra Yusuf Daoud, living in Los Angeles

Women in Afghanistan have long been portrayed as passive victims awaiting liberation. Following the attacks on New York on 11 September 2001, Washington, supported by London, used this as partial justification for a bombing campaign against Afghanistan. Thousands died in carpet bombing. After the fall of the Taliban, women were promised peace, security, development, democracy and liberation. US policy-makers characterized gender relations in Afghanistan in ways that legitimated their action. They made an analogy between the defeat of the Taliban and Al-Qaida, and women's liberation. Yet today, as under the Taliban, women in Afghanistan feel alienated as they face patriarchy and a lack of security and social and economic structures. Moreover, they have now found their culture under attack from an alien regime. Their world is full of anxiety as the social conditions which existed under the Taliban are being reconstituted and reproduced.

UNICEF has reported that at least one in two girls who should go to school remain at home, and one in five children do not survive long enough even to reach school age. Others will drop out of school to join the army of child labour, to support their families.[1] Worsening poverty has forced women into sex work; though it existed before the Taliban, since 2001 it has mushroomed to unprecedented levels. There has also been a dramatic rise in cases of self-immolation by women. The United Nations-backed Afghanistan Independent Human

Rights Commission (AIHRC) has pointed out that economic problems and widespread forced marriages are behind the increasing incidents of women committing suicide, especially in southern parts of Afghanistan where there is growing insurgency and poppy cultivation. Violence against women, including so-called honour killing, is also on the rise.[2] This happens despite the fact that women hold more than 25 per cent of the seats in the Afghan parliament and women's rights activists stand up to protest and defend women's rights; however, they often face intimidation and violence. Afghan authorities do not investigate women's complaints. Women's rights are not upheld and women's non-governmental organizations' (NGOs) workers are not protected and are being killed. In many ways this is not surprising, as known human rights abusers from the civil war (1992–96) and Taliban (1996–2001) periods have been appointed as law enforcers. Criminal warlords and commanders are a powerful faction in the parliament and, alongside a number of cabinet ministers, are deeply implicated in the drug businesses and civil strife.[3]

The International Security Assistance Force (ISAF), US and North Atlantic Treaty Organization (NATO) forces have no workable strategy to create a stable and peaceful Afghanistan as the devastation continues to worsen – due to large-scale drug cultivation, growing insurgency, crime and corruption. The peacekeeping mission of NATO is turning into a full-scale war against insurgents. NATO air strikes ruin houses and kill civilians. The Taliban and Al-Qaida are gaining public support due to the failure of the government and its western allies to provide security and development.[4]

Despite daily tragedies, Afghan women know how to struggle for their rights. They refused the gender identities that the Taliban attempted to impose and now they are refusing to conform to those imposed by invading forces. In their own way and according to their own culture, religion and ethnicity, they have been resisting the social control that the family and community try to impose on them. This, in essence, is the subject of this book. During the Taliban, in the diaspora and in Afghanistan today under foreign invasion, women's lives are shaped by gender power relations. *Afghan Women* centres on gender, agency and identity, and the extent to which men and women, through their engagement with violence, diasporic communities and with the invading forces, are agents for change.[5]

The stories I narrate in chapters 2, 3 and 4 are based on research carried out in interviews with women and men in Afghanistan, Iran, Pakistan, UK and USA.[6] Women's life histories are diverse but all have the common ground of a struggle against the gender prejudices ranged at them, from Islamic tradition to Orientalist representations.[7] These women are knowledgeable and empowered, they are aware of what the prevailing climate prevents them from doing but equally they are able to seize the opportunities that this climate creates. The knowledge garnered from these women's life histories is vital for an analytical understanding of the political, social and economic injustices which they face. All the names are fictitious, to respect the anonymity of those who discussed their life histories with me, unless they gave me permission to refer to them in their personal and institutional capacity. Speaking Farsi, which is spoken in Iran and resembles Dari spoken by the majority of Afghans, was an advantage and allowed me to discuss with Afghan women and men the reality of their lives which is different from the perception of Afghan women as passive victims of male and religious domination awaiting liberation by western values – an image which is too often portrayed in the West.

Gender, ethnicity, agency and identity

What gender actually means for Afghan women is vital to this book. Conventional gender divisions, as they have been understood in the West, fail to explain the fluidities of Afghan women's identities. Afghan women's agency and identity suggest a different view of gender, a greater fluidity in defining women and men so that they are not labelled merely by faith or gender. Throughout this book, Afghan women discuss gender in the context of social relations, Islamic religion, culture, domination, subordination and masculinity. They see gender as a process embedded in all social relations and institutions. It is a relationship that is constituted through their lived experience within continually redefined and contested social activities and institutions.[8]

Ethnic groups are particularly important to an understanding of gender in Afghanistan, although ethnicity itself is complex and variously defined by language, religion, descent, region and profession.[9] The Pashtuns are the largest ethnic group in Afghanistan, estimated to be 40 per cent of the population. They are based predominantly in the south and east of the country. They share the same norms and values as Pashtuns in north-west Pakistan and there is a great deal of solidarity between them. They are largely Sunni and have their own code of ethics known as *Pashtunwali* (Pashtuns' way of life) and their own language (Pashto). *Pashtunwali*, the customary law of the Pashtuns, is practised among eastern Pashtuns as part of their system of values and norms. According to *Pashtunwali,* it is the absolute duty of men to protect the respectability of women and to protect the integrity of the homeland. This does not imply that women stay passive. In Pashtun folklore, Malalai is praised for her decisive role in winning the battle of Mayward against the British in 1878–80. The Pashtun ethnic charter is based on patrilineality. However, sub-ethnic groups within Pashtuns, such as Afridi or Ghilzai, are connected to other Pashtuns through matrilineality. This history enables women, especially older women, to exercise power by practising *Pashtunwali* more strictly than men and being less ready to compromise when matters of honour of the family and community are at stake.[10]

Besides the Pashtuns in the east of Afghanistan, there are

Pashtuns who live in the west, in Kabul and other parts of Afghanistan and there is a significant minority of Shi'a Pashtuns in the Kandahar region. The traditional norms and values of these Pashtuns are more similar to those of other ethnic groups than to those of the Pashtuns in the east of Afghanistan. The concepts of honour and shame may be similar to *Pashtunwali* with its implied male domination and regulate gender relations in varying degrees, but these communities do not claim a specific ethnic monopoly over these norms and values as *Pashtunwali* does for the Pashtuns in east Afghanistan. The Tajiks constitute the second largest group in Afghanistan. They are Sunni and Dari speakers and are organized along local lineages, village clusters, valleys and occupational groups. They live in Kabul and other cities and identify with the geographical areas that they come from as well as their ethnicity. The Hazaras, who are predominantly Shi'a, are the third ethnic group. They live mainly in the central Afghan highlands known as Hazarajat and since the fall of the Taliban many Hazaras live in Kabul and Mazar Sharif. They speak a dialect of Persian known as Hazaragi. Some Hazaras are Sayids; they believe they are the descendants of the Prophet Muhammad; there are also Sunni and Ismaili Hazara minorities. Despite religious diversity, since the 1992 civil war Hazaras have become more united as one ethnic group. The Uzbeks are the fourth major ethnic group. They have lived in Afghanistan for centuries and were ruled by their own Emirs. Other Uzbeks migrated into Afghanistan after the expansion of Tsarist empire and during the Soviet expansion. They are mostly Sunni, live in the north of Afghanistan and speak their own Turkish language, although in the cities they also speak Dari. There are also many other smaller ethnic groups, cultures and languages.[11]

The diverse linguistic, cultural and ethnic identities in Afghanistan have been formed and reconstructed as a consequence of broader historical processes involving local and regional wars and colonial intervention. Within these identities, gender relations are not set in stone; they have evolved in the context of social struggles. Afghan history is characterized as much by conflicts arising from ethnic identities as by inter-ethnic relations through marriage which demonstrate very different principles of coexistence, harmony, tolerance and pride in diversity. Ethnic conflicts have predominantly been the result of ethnicized politics manipulated by leaders and foreign invaders.[12] Throughout the periods of civil war and Taliban rule, ethnic conflicts reached unprecedented levels. Hazaras were massacred in Kabul in 1994; Hazaras massacred the Taliban in Mazar-e-Sharif in 1997 and the Taliban massacred Hazaras and Uzbeks in 1998.[13] Yet despite high levels of ethnic conflict, women of diverse groups – Shi'a, Sunni, Pashtun, Tajik, Hazara and Uzbek – worked together in secret schools. In diaspora and under foreign invasion, women of different ethnicities and religions have been cooperating in the interest of their community as a whole.

Considering the importance of ethnicity in gender relations, the stories in this book highlight how women negotiate gender in different forms and how they sometimes find themselves in positions of domination, able to exercise power within the family and the community as well as subordination. As I will discuss in Chapter 2, the minority of pro-Taliban women exercised dominance over the majority of anti-Taliban women by supervising their work and persecuting them if they did not obey the Taliban's rule. Anti-Taliban women also broke one historical norm by observing another historical norm. They used the institutions of *mahram* (to be accompanied by their husbands or blood male relatives) and *chaddari* or *burqa* and hired men in their community and family to play the role of *mahram* for them. This way they exercised dominance over men by becoming their employers and demonstrated that where they are not submissive they are capable of behaving in a non-submissive manner.[14]

The solidarity and cooperation between women and men

enabled them to use *mahram* and *chaddari* as gender masks[15] to display the public submission of women to men and the public submission of women and men to Taliban women and men. Their material circumstances determined their survival strategy. Women were also empowered politically as they realized their ability to organize secret schools and gatherings and create networks of solidarity to save their communities from total disintegration.

Despite the horrifying conditions of life under the Taliban, Afghan women found a space in which to exercise autonomy and agency.[16] They broke the pre-defined spaces of confinement and silence and contested the idea that Muslim society is about building barriers to shut women out, condemning them to a life of domesticity and oppression. Afghan men also realized that gender solidarity was essential to their survival and the image of male domination, which is expected from them by ethnic and religious norms, was unrealistic and did not mean that they hold all the power while women are subordinate. Similarly, as I will discuss in Chapter 4 on the diaspora, Afghan women constantly struggle to break free from the confines of traditions, male domination and a life of marginalization, especially in Iran and Pakistan. Women do not consider their situation as being separate from that of men. They recognize that their needs and their demands are different from men's, but they see their lives as being affected by the same economic, social and political forces.

Contrary to popular views in the West, many Afghan men oppose traditional ideologies of male superiority and dominance. Therefore, I contest the common assumption that patriarchal ideologies are embedded much more strongly for Afghan men than they are for 'liberated' western men. I will also explore the challenges to masculine identity experienced by individual Afghan men and the varied ways in which they try to reconstruct their identity within the harsh realities of their lives under the Taliban, in diaspora and under foreign invasion.

Gender relations are, therefore, historically specific. They are determined by social, economic, class, political and legal as well as cultural and religious factors.[17]

In Afghanistan, as in all Muslim majority societies, the interaction of Islamic culture and religion with secularism, nationalism, ethnicity and other important historical, social and economic mechanisms structures the lives of women and men. Too often, Islamic culture and religion are considered to be the primary agent determining the identities of women in Muslim majority societies and are used to justify war, occupation and invasion. Of course, patriarchal attitudes and structures remain extremely strong in Afghanistan, but by discussing Afghan women's resistance and struggles against different structures of power (male, ethnic, religion, age, regional and international), I reject essentialisms about women in Afghanistan – and, indeed, in other Muslim majority societies. This book focuses on Afghan women's struggle to change the patriarchal gender relations which traditionally recognize only men as breadwinners, heads of household and decision-makers. I will argue that they have formed new and diverse conceptions concerning their identity and agency. They have been able to shape their own lives, histories and identities. Their struggles demonstrate that material conditions have important social and political consequences on their lives.[18]

As the writer of this book, I come from different identities and positions: an Iranian/British woman, university teacher, living in London, secular but deeply engaged with Iranian/Islamic culture. For twenty-five years, I have been involved with the women's movement in Iran and since 2001 with the anti-war movement in Britain. Therefore my identities, background, values and experiences have obviously shaped the way I understand and represent the experiences of Afghan women. My aim is to promote women's voices politically, socially and culturally, hoping that the voices of Afghan women in this book, representing many other voices, will be heard, enabling them to win their battle against both male domination and imperialist domination.

A short history

Afghanistan's history demonstrates how gender relations have been affected by ethnic conflict, state formation, state–society relations and imperial domination. In the nineteenth century, the British empire in the region was threatened by the expansion of the Russian empire. The British, therefore, attempted to conquer Afghanistan and did this through the manipulation of different ethnic groups. Afghanistan became a buffer state between these two empires, and successive monarchs ruled with no legitimacy as they subjugated the interest of the people of Afghanistan to foreign rule. For example, between 1881 and 1901 Abdur Rahman Khan, with the help of the British, ruthlessly crushed ethnic dissent and attempted to create a strong centralized state. The country's present borders were established according to the strategic needs of the imperial powers rather than the socio-political needs of Afghans' diverse groups. Subsequent ethnic conflicts and the backlash against modernization can be traced back to this period. In 1893 an agreement was signed between Abdur Rahman Shah and Mortimer Durand, the foreign secretary of the colonial government of India. As part of this agreement, the Durand Line was drawn to mark the boundary between Afghanistan and the British Indian empire. In 1947, following the partition of India, it became the border between Pakistan and Afghanistan. This line, which runs through Pashtun areas, even to this day has never been recognized by the Pashtuns in these two countries; periodically, the issue of an independent state of Pashtunistan is raised.[19]

In 1901, Abdur Rahman Khan died, his son Habibullah succeeded him and took steps towards modernization. After the First World War, resistance to British interference grew. Habibullah was assassinated and his son Amanullah Khan seized power, declaring independence in 1919. The British colonial intrusion (1880–1919) was followed by rivalries between the Pashtun and non-Pashtun ethnic groups, when successive Pashtun rulers redistributed resources in favour of Pashtuns and to the detriment of other ethnicities. The power-holders used one ethnic group against another to divide and rule. King Amanullah introduced a limited degree of reforms such as land reform, trade, tax collection, improving infrastructure, provision of healthcare and education and a degree of women's rights. However, the constitution, which was proclaimed in 1923, was abrogated in 1924, because only a very few people benefited from its reforms, and the weak rentier state, surviving on foreign grants and loans, remained unpopular with the majority of the people. King Amanullah was overthrown. Nadir Shah, who became the next monarch, consolidated his rule by making concessions to religious conservatism and hierarchy and the 1931 constitution omitted any mention of women's rights.[20] Following Nadir, his son Zahir Shah (1933–73) once again attempted reform, including a new secular constitution of 1964, provision of education for women and an end to sex segregation by voluntary removal of the veil. But, in the end, he too was overthrown for being unable to alleviate poverty and the 1972 famine during which 100,000 Afghans died.[21]

In 1973, Mohammed Daoud took power and dissolved the monarchy. Yet, like his predecessors, he failed to build institutions according to the needs of Afghanistan's diverse society; instead, he created a large bureaucracy and relied on economic and military aid from the Soviet Union and the USA, but failed to bring benefits to the majority of the population. In 1978, he was overthrown by the People's Democratic Party of Afghanistan (PDPA) and the Democratic Republic of Afghanistan was established. The pro-Soviet rulers in this period were divided into two factions, the Khalg (Masses) and the Parcham (Flag). They attempted a number of reforms from land reform to the reform of family laws as well as the provision of healthcare and education for women. But because of their lack of understanding of the complexities of Afghan society and because they did not extend the benefits to the majority of the population, there was a widespread rural revolt against them. Nancy Tapper suggests that the reform of family law in this period was not much different from the reforms of earlier regimes since the 1880s, in the sense that none of these reforms resolved the harsh reality of the majority of the people and all were formulated by the male Afghan elite, based on western models.[22] Similarly, Nazif Shahrani notes that the uprising during the 1978–79 rebellion was aimed against the regime with strong ties to the Soviet Union rather than simply against women's rights and a modernizing state.[23] In 1979, Soviet troops invaded Afghanistan, the Cold War intensified and Afghan Mujaheddin became the US-backed anti-Soviet force. For the majority of Afghans, the Soviet invasion was yet another foreign interference in their country.

In the post-Second World War period, the United States replaced Britain as a global superpower and its influence on Iran, Central Asia and China intensified, competing with the Soviet Union as the other emerging superpower.[24] In the 1960s and 1970s, middle- and upper-class women in Kabul had access to education and employment and moved freely around the city without *chaddari* and *mahram*. During the Soviet invasion, women in Kabul and a few other major cities worked as scientists, pharmacists, teachers, medical doctors and civil servants.[25] These, however, were a small minority of urban women who enjoyed considerable freedom of movement, educational opportunities and a relatively wide range of career choices, in contrast to the majority of women in urban and rural areas who lived in poverty and were excluded from this emancipatory process favouring urban areas, certain classes and ethnic groups.[26] Only a very small segment of the population, primarily government officials, army officers and the urban merchant class, who were also well represented in the government bureaucracy, benefited economically and politically. The majority of rural people and urban poor were not affected by the process of development. Those in power did not represent the majority. Their principal policy was one of divide and rule. Women's rights issues were formulated by the predominantly male Afghan elite and were generally based on western models of women's rights which were culturally insensitive and unpopular with the majority of Afghan women. In this period, a minority of intellectual women were involved with the women's movements. They were the privileged few in the urban areas who had gained access to education and healthcare. The rural and urban areas were a world apart.[27] Zohra Yusuf Daoud became Miss Afghanistan in 1972, not a western-type 'Miss' in a swimsuit competition, but the winner of an intelligence competition, and was given the opportunity to travel to big cities like Herat, Mazar-e-Sharif and Kandahar to promote the country's literacy programme. During her trip she witnessed abject poverty, illiteracy and jails full of women who had run away from forced marriages:

> Although all women had the right to vote, not all women were allowed to exercise this right. Although theoretically women had the choice not to wear a veil, not all women were permitted to make that choice. Although theoretically every Afghan woman had a chance of an education, not all women could seize that opportunity. Islam wasn't keeping these women from moving forward; the traditionalists and their cultures were women's greatest obstacles in their quest for equality.[28]

These women questioned the religious leaders who told them the Qur'an gives a husband the right to beat his wife. But they found themselves isolated, as the majority of women could not identify with these movements and associated them with foreign domination and humiliation. They tried their best to persuade women and their fathers and husbands that women have the right to be educated. They were the same men who, though the state policy officially advocated reforms, simultaneously, as heads of their families, imposed traditional gender relations. It was not just men; often, older women gave the traditional explanation that this is 'how things have always been, and there is nothing anyone can do about it'.[29] Women were successful only if they quoted from the Qur'an in praise of the value of education and showed that the Qur'an does not advocate a hierarchy in which men are placed above women. They found this approach effective, and some men allowed their wives and daughters to be educated.[30]

The structure of the book

Chapter 2 discusses Afghan women and their lives under the civil war and the Taliban. During the period of Taliban rule, many women in Kabul and other parts of Afghanistan risked their lives by turning their homes into underground organizations for women and children. They created cohesion and solidarity in their communities. These networks and forms of solidarity became mechanisms for women's empowerment. The chapter will demonstrate how violent conflict during the Taliban era affected women and men differently and how women's secret organizations resisting the Taliban regime enabled them to prove their strength, pulling themselves from the depths of seclusion and oppression to reach a free space of agency. Furthermore, it reveals the way in which many Afghan men refused to participate in raping, killing and violating women and instead stood by women and supported their secret organizations.

Chapter 3 discusses the challenges facing women and men in Afghanistan in the years 2001 to 2007, under foreign invasion. The social capital which women built under the Taliban regime seems to have been crucial for the process of reconstruction. Many individuals and groups of western-educated women and men have returned to Afghanistan to help with the reconstruction of their country. But they face the rise of warlordism, the opium economy and a lack of meaningful progress. The insecurity, armed conflict and harsh economic conditions have forced many to return to Iran and Pakistan. I will argue that the presence of international organizations, international financial institutions, donor governments, UN agencies, international NGOs, the private sector and the military weakens the possibility of nation-state-building in Afghanistan. The efforts of the international community, based on imported western notions of market liberalization, governance and gender mainstreaming, are failing to bring about state-building, peace and security.

Chapter 4 is a comparative analysis of the diversity and commonality of Afghan women's and men's experiences in diasporic communities in Iran, Pakistan, the UK and USA. Women's stories reveal their commitment to changing patriarchal gender relations according to their own cultural diversity. The experience of the women's movement in Iran, and the efforts of a number of NGOs in Iran and Pakistan, have provided tremendous support for Afghan women's struggle and resistance. In contrast, Afghan women in the UK and USA do not see themselves as part of the western feminist movement. I look at their different experiences of refugee and immigrant status in surrounding countries and in the West. In particular, I look at how they have negotiated their identities in these very different contexts and their commitment to diversity and reinvesting gender relations.

In Chapter 5, the conclusion of this book, I will argue that the future of women's rights in Afghanistan depends not only on overcoming local male domination, but also on challenging imperial domination and bridging the growing divide between the West and the Muslim world. Afghan women's struggle is against imperial domination as much as it is against male domination. This has powerful implications, not only for dominant western narratives of saving Afghan women from religious oppression, it also calls for a wider feminist reconceptualization of women's rights and democracy in the context of imperialism and invasion.

Notes

1 UNICEF 2006: www.rawa.org/UNICEF.htm

2 Afghanistan Independent Human Rights Commission, 2006: www.aihrc.org.af and www.rawa.org/wom.ihrc.htm

3 *Daily Telegraph*, 5 February 2006: www.rawa.org/drugs

4 *Washington Post*, 30 May 2006: www.rawa.org

5 For this discussion, see also Rostami-Povey 2007a: 295–310 and 2007b: 242–61.

6 For the details of my field research, which includes forty-eight individual and thirty-three group interviews with 180 women and twenty men, see my end of award report, on the Economic Social Research Council (ESRC) Society Today website as a record of the research I undertook with ESRC funds: www.esrcsocietytoday.ac.uk/esrcinfocentre

7 Edward Said (1979 and 1993) pioneered the discussion about Orientalism as a mode of representing, and misrepresenting, the Islamic world as a domain of otherness and inferiority.

8 For an important discussion of interconnectedness of gender with other factors, see Harzig 2003: 50; and Afshar 1989: 211–25.

9 Simonsen 2004: 708–11.

10 Glatzer 2002: 265–82; 2001: 375–95; 1998: 167–81.

11 Ibid.

12 Monsutti 2005: 77–82; Barakat and Wardell 2001: 53.

13 Rashid 2001: 11.

14 For this discussion, see Scott 1990: 3; Harris's study of women in Tajikistan (2004) and my study of women in Iran (Poya 1999).

15 This is the term used by Scott 1990; and Harris 2004.

16 For discussions on agency and women's agency, see Orlando 1999: 139; Stewart and Strathern 2000: 61 and 122; Long 1992: 5 and 23; Moser and Clark 2001: 13–30; Momsen and Kinnaird 1993; Parpart and Marchand 1995: 3.

17 For this discussion, see Buijs 1993: 55.

18 For an excellent discussion of diaspora identity, including gender identity, see Bujis 1993; Indra 1989: 221–42 and 2003; Lenz et al. 2002; Said 1993: 15.

19 Rubin 1995; Johnson and Leslie 2004: 138; Rashid 2000: 10; Barakat and Wardell 2001: 138.

20 Kandiyoti 2005: 5.

21 Rubin 1995; Johnson and Leslie 2004: 139–40.

22 Tapper 1984: 12–15.

23 Shahrani 1984: 9–10.

24 Barakat and Wardell 2001: 5.

25 Dupree 1998; Barakat and Wardell 2001: 11–30.

26 Barakat and Wardell 2001.

27 Yusuf Daoud 2002: 103–4.

28 Ibid.

29 Vorgetts 2002: 94–7.

30 Ibid.

2 | Resistance and struggle under the Taliban

> ن دی د دننام دوب یک ندینش
>
> 'Shenidan Kay Bovad Manande Didan' (It is one thing to hear about something, but quite another to see it with your own eyes). Suraya Parlyka, Kabul

Afghan history is peppered with strong and heroic women. In the tenth century, Rabia Balkhi was the first woman to write love poetry in Persian. She died after her brother slashed her wrists for sleeping with a slave lover and she is reputed to have written her last poem in her own blood as she lay dying. (When the Taliban captured Mazar-e-Sharif, where her tomb lies, they placed it out of bounds as a mark of respect.) In the nineteenth century, Malali led troops into battle against the British.[1]

The women's movement in the twentieth century kept alive this tradition. In the 1960s, in particular, a minority of women played important roles. Their views and activities were diverse: Anahita Ratib became a member of parliament in 1965 and Minister of Social Affairs in 1977 under the pro-Soviet government; in 1994, Fatima Gailani was a member of the guerrilla army of the Afghan Resistance against the Soviets. Under the Taliban, the women's hospital in Kabul was named Rabia Balkhi and, for the first time, women doctors practised surgery, because only female doctors were allowed to attend female patients. The Revolutionary Association of the Women of Afghanistan (RAWA), established in 1977 to struggle for democracy, women's rights and human rights, chose Malali's name for their hospital in Quetta in Pakistan and for years provided medical care to Afghan refugee women and children. RAWA published *Payam-e Zan*, a quarterly political magazine, and since 1979 have engaged in resistance to war. Meena Keshwar Kamal, the founding member of RAWA, was assassinated in 1987 by conservative commanders and warlords[2] who opposed women's rights.[3]

During the Taliban regime, although ethnic conflict was at its highest level, women of diverse ethnic and religious groups worked together. The majority of women fought against the Taliban; a minority colluded with the Taliban. In different ways they exercised agency and identity.

Communal identity and gender relations

In Afghan society, community and group identity dominates. In rural areas in particular, the concept of individual identity is non-existent. Even in urban areas and among the educated upper and middle classes, as well as among the diaspora communities in the West, communal identity is strong. This communal identity has an enormous impact on gender relations. Women see themselves as an integral part of the family unit shaped by Afghan culture and tradition. They do not see their needs as separate from the needs of their families. Thus, traditional gender relations are complex. Women tend to be highly respected within the family and community. Traditionally, women are peace-brokers as well as mobilizing resistance among communities. In rural areas in particular, women are responsible for signalling the end of hostilities and the beginning of peaceful coexistence between competing tribes.[4]

Women's contribution to the economy is undeniable and is based on communal labour in agriculture and cooperation with men. Historically, sowing, ploughing and heavy harvesting tasks are performed by men and the remaining harvesting tasks are performed by women. Rural women manage domestic food supplies and determine what should be sold as cash crops and what should be retained to feed the family. Carpet weaving has been an important part of the rural economy. Men herd and shear the sheep; women spin the wool into yarn; men dye the wool; women weave the carpets; and men sell the carpets in the market. Women in rural areas have also been involved with animal husbandry.[5] However, despite high respect for women and their important contribution to the economy, when marrying, a woman moves into the home of her husband; there exists a very strong Afghan code of honour which dictates that, once married, an Afghan man must protect and care for his wife. A woman's status increases significantly once she produces children, while childlessness is regarded as disastrous for both men and women. At another level, the practice of exchanging girls and young women to settle tribal feuds or to repay debts remains ingrained.[6]

Gender segregation is a key part of this communal setting. Women socialize with women and men socialize with men. It is also a part of the family and community code of honour which advocates the cultural practice of masculine protection of women. Gender segregation is in the context of the institution of *mahram* which places relationships between the sexes in two categories: *mahram* relationships, which are formed either by birth or by marriage; and *namahram*, the opposite, that is, men with whom women are not permitted to interact. Hence, women have to be accompanied by a *mahram* in public. Another form of segregation is the covering of the female body. Women's mobility in urban centres is determined by the practice of *mahram* and *chaddari*, or other forms of cover depending on ethnic identity. In rural areas women do not wear *chaddari*, unless they travel to the cities. They wear different forms of cover including scarves embroidered according to the traditional specificities of different ethnic groups. These also differ in size, some just cover the hair and the head and others cover the whole body.[7] However, Afghanistan history demonstrates that communal identity and gender relations are not static and absolute; they are constructs which are negotiated and changed as they encounter socio-economic and political changes, especially changes in power relations within the family and the community.

The history of the country illustrates that the failure of

development efforts and women's rights issues was not simply the result of the contradiction between modernity and tradition; it was the result of the widening gap between the urban elite and the urban and rural majority. As this gap grew, leaders lost respect and credibility. In the face of corruption and oppression, communities turned to local leaders and created a power structure parallel to the central government to deal with their grievances.[8] Gender issues and women's rights in Afghanistan can be addressed only in the context of socio-economic development, peace and security. Constitutional and judicial reforms imposed from above and from outside are not sustainable without the provision of healthcare, education and employment for all women in rural and urban areas alike and the involvement of ordinary women themselves. Furthermore, in the absence of socio-economic development and state building, ethnic conflicts escalated throughout the twentieth century. Years of war and conflict strengthened local identity. Solidarity within different ethnic groups strengthened the position of commanders and warlords.[9] Traditionally, care and support of the vulnerable are deeply embedded within Afghan culture and, in times of need, most Afghans turn to family and the community for support. However, years of war and conflict have destroyed this communal security and eroded the family and community support mechanisms that have provided the principal coping strategy for most. People became increasingly vulnerable and resorted to desperate strategies for coping. Men joined with warlords and later the Taliban, boys became involved in child labour and child soldiering. Women and girls, separated from their families by conflict, displacement and migration, turned to begging and sex work.

The civil war and the Taliban period

To understand the plight of Afghan women under the Taliban, it is important to understand why and how the Taliban came to power. In the 1980s, the Soviet Union poured US$45 billion dollars into Afghanistan and the USA committed US$5 billion aid to the Mujaheddin. In addition, Afghanistan received another $10 billion from European countries, Saudi Arabia, Pakistan and other countries in the region. In 1998, Zbigniew Brzezinski, US National Security Adviser (1977–81) under President Jimmy Carter, admitted that the CIA has been instructed to give secret aid to the Mujaheddin. After 9/11, when asked whether he regretted supporting the Mujaheddin, he replied:

> Regret what? The secret operation was an excellent idea. It had the effect of drawing the Russians into the Afghan trap and you want me to regret it? The day that the Soviets officially crossed the border I wrote to President Carter: we now have the opportunity of giving the USSR its own Vietnam War ... What is more important to the history of the world? The Taliban or the collapse of the Soviet empire? A few crazed Muslims or the liberation of Central Europe and the end of the Cold War?[10]

Yet, this support for the Mujaheddin led to a brutal civil war (1992–96) in which 1.5 million Afghans died, 7 million were displaced and the country was devastated. While the USA saw the collapse of the Soviet Union as the failure of the communist regime, many Muslims saw it as a victory for Islam. Shirmohammed who lived in Afghanistan during this period explained to me how Afghans felt betrayed by the West:

> The US and western governments wanted the complete defeat of the Soviet Union and not the liberation of Afghanistan. In fact they sacrificed Afghanistan for their own agenda. They did not strengthen the position of nationalists and the seculars in Afghanistan; they strengthened the Islamic fanatics and anarchy, including the coming to power of Bin Laden, Al-Qaida and later the Taliban. The West was responsible for the civil war.

Indeed, the war against the Soviet invasion had a devastating impact on the rural population and the economy. Cities were also destroyed. Millions were internally displaced and millions took refuge in neighbouring countries, mainly Iran and Pakistan. With the collapse of the state, the aid community increasingly performed the role of a surrogate state, providing food, healthcare and education. A number of women worked for the aid agencies and also continued carpet weaving and handicraft production.[11] The country's industrial base was, and still is, limited to small-scale production of textiles, soap, furniture, shoes, fertilizer, cement, hand-woven carpets, gas, oil, coal and copper. The civil war had a devastating impact on economic activities. Widespread asset stripping and privatization of public assets by the Mujaheddin led to a drastic fall in the living standards of people in urban areas who relied on the state sector as the main employer of the majority of the population. Opium production increased as a means of surviving the rural and urban destruction and poverty. Violence, especially against women, escalated to an unprecedented level. Young women were raped and killed and their bodies were dumped in graveyards. No one dared to oppose them. Parvana, a university student in Mazar-e-Sharif in this period, explained:

> This was a very difficult period. We could not study because hundreds and thousands of internally displaced people from Kabul and other cities were coming to take refuge in Mazar-e-Sharif and we were engaged in turning schools and universities into temporary homes for them. It was terrible to hear from these refugees how brother is killing brother, neighbour killing another neighbour because people were fighting for different factions and different commanders and warlords. My mother was worried about me continuing to go to university. But my father left it to me to decide. There were times that I was the only woman in the university. The warlords were pressurizing my father to force me to wear *chaddari*. But my father always told them that I have the courage to go out without *chaddari*. At the time I was working for the local newspaper in Balkh. Towards the end I was the only woman who was working in the

media in our area. It was not just me, many women till the last moment worked and went to university.

According to Islamic law, women should not be forced into marriage; their consent is always necessary. Where a minor has been married without this, she can ask for her marriage to be annulled on reaching the age of majority. Despite this law, commanders and warlords forced women to marry them against their will and consent.

Support for the Mujaheddin also led to the emergence of Osama Bin Laden as the leader of al-Qaida. Bin Laden was a Saudi businessman, wealthy and close to the Saudi royal family. In 1980 he met with Mujaheddin leaders and with CIA funding he built a major arms storage depot, and training and medical centres for the Mujaheddin. He and other Arab militants allied with the extremist Pashtun Mujaheddin, alienating the non-Pashtuns and Shi'a ethnic and religious groups. However, by 1990 he was disillusioned by factions fighting within the Mujaheddin and left Afghanistan. Following the first Gulf War in 1991, US troops entered Saudi Arabia and Bin Laden began criticizing Saudi Arabia's close relationship with the USA; he was no longer an ally of the USA. According to the CIA, Bin Laden sponsored terrorist camps and activities in Somalia, Egypt, Sudan, Yemen, Kenya, Tanzania, Riyadh, Dhahran, Aden, Afghanistan and the World Trade Center in 1993. Only at this stage was he declared to be a terrorist but the USA never admitted that years of sponsoring Afghan Mujaheddin had created these movements across the Muslim world with grievances against their own American-backed rulers. In 1996, Bin Laden returned to Afghanistan under the protection of the Taliban. Washington continued to ignore Afghanistan, the civil war and the rule of the Taliban until the events of 9/11.[12]

The Taliban grew out of the discontent of many of the younger generation of Mujaheddin who felt that their older leadership had failed; people were suffering from death, rape and destruction. They began to search for a solution and decided on a programme of restoring peace, enforcing strict Shari'a law and disarming the population. The majority were students in *madrassas* (religious schools) and chose the name Taliban (religious students) to distance themselves from the party politics of the Mujaheddin and to signal that they were a movement for cleansing society of war and unIslamic behaviour. Thousands of young male teenagers who had spent their lives in refugee camps in Pakistan joined the Taliban. They had never seen their country at peace and had no knowledge of its complex ethnic identities. Many were orphans who had grown up without mothers and sisters in the confines of segregated male refugee camps and the *madrassa* system where only war and a puritanical Islam gave meaning to their lives.[13]

The Taliban's leaders came from the poorest, the least literate and the most conservative Pashtun areas in the southern provinces of Afghanistan. Their treatment of women was based on the conservative norms and values of *Pashtunwali* that they had absorbed in the *madrassas* rather than on the Shari'a law. They were determined to impose *Pashtunwali* on other ethnic groups by force. This deepened the ethnic divide in the country.[14] Yet it is important to recognize that Pashtuns are a diverse ethnic group. The Pashtuns in the eastern provinces of Afghanistan were influenced by the Pakistani Pashtuns and were proud to send their girls to school. During the Taliban rule these Pashtuns sent their families, including girls and young women, to be educated in Pakistan. Also *Pashtunwali* is not just about punishment; it includes many positive norms and values of the Pashtuns, including hospitality.[15]

Throughout the periods of civil war (1992–96) and Taliban rule (1996–2001) ethnic conflicts reached unprecedented levels. By mid-2001 the Taliban controlled more than 90 per cent of Afghanistan and imposed their rules on the Afghan people. By this time they had managed to impose relative peace and security. They disarmed the once heavily armed population and controlled opium production. Aid led to the expansion of trade and the monetization of the economy.[16] In rural areas, women continued to contribute to the functioning of the rural economy; however, in the cities the Taliban drastically curtailed women's access to education and work.[17] The creation of the institution of al-Amr bi-al-ma.ruf wa-al-nahy an almunkar (the promotion of virtue and prevention of vice) had a devastating impact on women's mobility. It policed the Taliban's gender policy, which was declared as a decree:

> Women, you should not step outside your residence. If you go outside the house you should not be like women who used to go with fashionable clothes wearing cosmetics and appearing in front of every man before the coming of Islam. Islam as a rescuing religion has determined specific dignity for women, Islam has valuable instructions for women. Women should not create such opportunity to attract the attention of useless people who will not look at them with a good eye. Women have the responsibility as a teacher or coordinator for her family. Husband, brother, father have the responsibility for providing the family with the necessary life requirements (food, clothes etc). In case women are required to go outside the residence for the purpose of education, social needs or social services they should cover themselves in accordance with Islamic Shari'a regulation. If women are going outside with fashionable, ornamental and charming clothes to show themselves, they will be cursed by the Islamic Shari'a and should never expect to go to heaven. All family elders and every Muslim have responsibility in this respect. We request all family elders to keep tight control over their families and avoid these social problems. Otherwise these women will be threatened, investigated and severely punished as well as the family elders by the forces of the Religious Police. The Religious Police have the responsibility and duty to struggle against these social problems and will continue their effort until evil is finished.[18]

During the civil war, schools were destroyed. Thus the Taliban's gender policies only worsened an ongoing crisis. Illiteracy was a major problem before the Taliban, affecting 90 per cent of girls and 60 per cent of boys. Within three months of the capture of Kabul in 1996, the Taliban closed schools and Kabul University, affecting hundreds of thousands of female students and teachers. Najia described the situation in her home: 'My daughters were crying saying that, as their mother, I went to university, now they cannot even go to school. But I gave them hope that one day things will be better, they just have to be patient.'

Education for boys was also at a standstill in Kabul because most of the teachers were women, who could not work. In this period, US government aid funds were designated for the education of Afghan girls and excluded boys. The lack of education for boys drove many Afghan families to resort to the only recourse available – the *madrassas*, hothouses of indoctrination and fertile recruiting grounds for child soldiers.[19]

Throughout the 1990s, the UN humanitarian aid programme to Afghanistan was reduced drastically. As a result, children died of simple, preventable diseases because there were no health facilities and no clean water. Women had to cope with no food and children became malnourished. The whole population suffered from trauma and depression. Every norm of family life had been destroyed by the war. Most children had witnessed extreme violence, death, mutilated bodies and had lost at least one family member. They suffered from nightmares and depression and a lack of trust in adults who could not protect them.[20] Somayeh, an Iranian voluntary worker with Médecins Sans Frontières (MSF), working in the border area between Iran and Afghanistan with internally displaced Afghans, described the situation as follows:

> Many had forgotten the basic things in life such as brushing their hair, washing, eating properly and even using the toilet

> for going to toilet. I sometimes played with the children and made them cheerful, they ate better. I held them, kissed them and told them jokes. They responded positively. Many parents were saying that they forgot how to do these things with their children. There was a woman who everybody said was mad. But I discovered that she was not mad, she just needed affection. No one was touching her, because she was very dirty and covered in dirt and mud. I held her and kissed her. She cried, I cried and she started talking and later she cleaned herself and ate her food.

The experiences of Afghan women under the Taliban

Restrictive policies were applied in all Taliban-controlled areas, but their impact was felt most acutely in Kabul, Mazar-e-Sharif, Heart and other Dari-speaking urban centres where women had traditionally enjoyed a greater degree of freedom than in the more conservative Pashtun heartland cities of Kandahar and Jalalabad. Najia said:

> Even a small minority of educated women and middle-class women were forced to marry the Taliban. I know of an educated woman who was the head of the school of medicine at the university and was forced to marry the Taliban. They were either forced or did it out of poverty or fear. Sometimes a woman who was married to one Taliban was raped by ten other Taliban. Sometimes they were taken to outside of Afghanistan, especially to the Gulf region and were sold as sex workers.

In some ways women's situation was worse during the civil war than during Taliban rule. This is because so many women were murdered and raped by the Mujaheddin. The Taliban disarmed the commanders and warlords and brutally enforced their own model of law and order. They imposed the *chaddari* on women and punished those women who did not obey its law. Guita explained:

> Sometimes they would beat women in the streets and nobody could do anything. People just stood and watched. They had a stick with lead at the end of it to beat women to cover themselves. It was difficult to see through the *chaddari*. When we went shopping we couldn't see what we were buying. If we put the *chaddari* up to see, they would hit us and close the shop. So shop keepers were not selling things to women.

Under the Taliban, thousands of female-headed households, who were internally displaced, lived in refugee camps around cities, most of their husbands having been killed during the civil war years and under Taliban rule. They are called *Zanane bee Sarparast* (unprotected women), a derogatory term. A section of the Refugee Centre in Kabul was reserved specifically for them where, separated from the other households, they lived as a separate community. Saghar said:

> During the Taliban, and after, we received less food than other households from the aid agencies. This is because many of us were not, and even now after the fall of Taliban are not, registered and do not possess an official card to receive help. Also there is no soap or cleansing materials and we suffer more than men because of our monthly menstruation period. We produce handicrafts and sell them to raise some money for ourselves and our children.

Women, men and children suffered from malnutrition and various diseases. There were also specific health problems deriving from the war, both physical and psychological. Years of repression, deprivation and dire socio-economic conditions have severely affected the mental well-being of the majority of citizens. As Suraya Parlyka, head of the National Union of Women of Afghanistan, explained: 'We all suffer from the psychological pains of the war and destruction. It is going to take a long time to reduce and cure the pains of Afghan women, especially the female-headed households and the orphanages.'

Women often burst into tears when they talk about their losses. For example, this is what Zakera had to say:

> I was a school teacher; I lost my leg and my arm when a bomb went off eight years ago, during the civil war. Despite this I got married and had two children. My older son was born with a heart problem linked to the incident, which gives me recurring nightmares. Some members of my family, friends, and neighbours believe that it was a good thing that I got married and had children; others think that I should not have. I don't know what is wrong and what is right. Sometimes I feel like committing suicide.

Suhaila, a journalist, had similar feelings: 'My three brothers were killed during the civil war and under Taliban rule; this is a terrible loss.' A woman in the Kabul Refugee Centre also expressed her sense of loss: 'I was not a poor woman, I had a nice home, [but] we lost everything. Years of unemployment, war and destruction led me to go begging in order to feed myself and my children.' Many women had no choice but sell their bodies to feed themselves and their children. Inter-familial violence against women, the low social status of women, and the consequent power imbalances between women and men that it generates, became the norm. Despite terrifying conditions under the Taliban, Afghan women pulled themselves from the depth of seclusion and oppression and found a space to exercise autonomy and agency.[21]

Women's survival strategies

Survival strategies are deeply embedded in the material conditions of life. It is usually the poorer sections of society that remain in the war-stricken areas during times of violent conflict, while those with economic opportunities usually migrate elsewhere. However, significant minorities of professional women remained in Afghanistan or have returned to their country. For these women, survival strategies were based on forming networks and groups in solidarity with poorer women. This way they built the foundation for creating social capital[22] which was essential for their survival. By creating networks of trust and reciprocity in their neighbourhoods, among their friends and relatives they gave cohesion to their communities. Under Taliban rule, these networks and forms of solidarity became mechanisms for women's empowerment.

Many prominent women chose to stay in Afghanistan and work, either openly or clandestinely, towards empowering other women (as well as children). For example, Suraya Parlyka, as head of the National Union of Women of Afghanistan, became an integral part of the women's movement:

> We witnessed twenty-two years of war, terror and bombing. We have an ancient saying, *Shenidan Kay Bovad Manande Didan* (It is one thing to hear about something, but quite another to see it with your own eyes). Under the Mujaheddin, the weapon of one community against another was to attack, to jail, to rape, to hit in public the female members of the other community. Under the Taliban, women were denied their basic right to education. Throughout, we continued our activities, openly and secretly, and this allowed us to hold hands with each other and survive. Both during the civil war and under the Taliban committing suicide was widespread amongst women. Under the Taliban, we tried to stop women committing suicide when their families imposed forced marriages on them. We advised women not to fight their families, pretend that they will accept and near the time to escape and come to us for protection. We saved a large number of women this way. We organized carpet weaving and other skills and women were able to survive this way.

Other examples abound. The non-governmental Women's Vocational Training Centre was active for twenty years and offered women in Kabul classes in English and German as well as computer-skills courses. Its activists also provided courses in handicrafts, animal husbandry, bee-keeping and honey-making in rural areas outside Kabul. They created income-generating activities for women. Shafiqa, the director, told me:

> We had 6,000 students from seven to thirty-five years of age. When the Taliban came to power, they closed down our institution. But we continued our underground activities in our homes. Many times we were threatened with imprisonment and torture, but we continued. It was very difficult for men as well. Men also had problems if they wanted to work. They had to grow beard and hair to a particular length, and there were no jobs for them to do. In some ways, it was easier for women. Wearing *chaddari* allowed us to do some work.

Ghamar, another active member of this organization, also explained how the group was attempting to include children who face social exclusion because of their different forms of disability: 'there are a large number of children who are blind, deaf and/or maimed because of the civil war. We tried to teach them different skills, and include them in our projects according to their abilities.'

Under Taliban rule, the Women's Association of Afghanistan funded and managed secret sewing, knitting and handicraft courses for women. Shafiqa, a leading member of this organization, explained: 'These courses took place in the homes of the teachers. Sometimes we had to change our venue for fear of persecution by the Taliban, but we continued. Our activities enabled many women to make clothes and other necessities for themselves and their families, and sometimes they sold or exchanged their products with other women.'

The doctors in the Rabia Balkhi Women's Hospital were all educated in Kabul. Setting up the hospital had the advantage of allowing these women to perform surgery. According to Dr Rahima, the hospital manager 'Surgery was the domain of male doctors. During Taliban rule, only female doctors were allowed to attend to female patients. Throughout this period we remained in Afghanistan and worked in the hospital with barely minimum facilities and without being paid. We did it to serve our people and the poorest of the poor in our country.'

Mahbuba Hoquqmal, a woman lawyer who in 2001 became state Minister for Women, taught law at the University of Kabul before Taliban rule. Under the Taliban, she moved to Peshawar and worked with women's NGOs on gender legal issues. 'In my profession I learnt how women in Afghanistan are denied many rights. Under the Taliban, even the basic rights to education were taken away from them. My aim is to raise these issues in Afghanistan and at the international level to make women aware of their rights and to change the legal position of women in Afghanistan.'

Saddiqa Balkhi, who became Minister for the Disabled in 2003, under the Taliban was the head of the Islamic Centre for Political and Cultural Activities of Afghan Women. She was a teacher. She left Afghanistan in 1981 and went to Khorasan in north-east Iran.

> A large number of Afghan people migrated to Iran, I therefore decided to go and work with refugee women. We set up schools for Afghan women and provided opportunities for different groups of women to be in touch with each other. In cooperation with United Nations High Commissioner for Refugees (UNHCR) in Iran, we identified 2,500 female-headed households in Mashhad, the capital city of Khorasan, [although] I am sure there were many more that we did not reach. We managed to set up courses for these women and provided opportunities for them to be involved in income-generating activities.

Balkhi returned to Afghanistan in 1991 and continued her work with women in Mazar-e-Sharif, Herat, Kandahar and Kabul.

Fatana Gailani was and still is the head of Afghan Women Council (AWC). She set up a school and hospital for women in Peshawar. Nasira, who was working with AWC, explained her activities to me:

> Several times I travelled to Afghanistan; my responsibility was to help the widows who were the head of their families. They had to work to earn money, but they couldn't because the Taliban did not allow women to go to work. I went to their houses and helped them. We also published a newspaper called *Afghan Women*. We wrote about women and their problems. We tried to talk to them about how to cope and try to take control of their lives as much as they could. We published the paper in Pakistan and I took them to Afghanistan and distributed them to the women. We tried to help them by creating work for them. We asked them to do what they can, such as needlework, sewing, knitting, and paid them salary. We also encouraged them to study in the secret schools.

Poverty in Afghanistan is predominantly the result of war and the collapse of economic activity. Even middle-class and educated women experienced poverty. They worked in their homes, teaching, knitting, sewing, producing and exchanging goods and services. Had they not done this, they would have been in the streets begging. Many poorer women with fewer skills were begging and some became sex workers. Networking and group solidarity enabled these women to survive and help other women who lived under extreme forms of poverty and possessed few skills, or who had lost their male head of household; many of these women had no choice but to become beggars or sex workers. Leila said, 'During Taliban we only received food and clothes from our female neighbours.' As the basis of their daily coping strategies, these poor women relied only on women's support networks to meet their bare necessities.

Despite the horrors of war and violent conflict, some women in Afghanistan emerged from such times empowered. They became aware of their own capacities to organize and found ways to survive. Women's secret organizations and networks in Afghanistan were the only functioning organizations trusted by the community.

Some women's experiences of conflict resulted in their learning skills and obtaining social, economic and political exposure and strength. In effect, conflicts extended beyond the battlefield and into the domains of everyday life. A great many women school and university teachers were engaged in teaching girls, young women and some boys in their neighbourhoods. Some taught between ten and sixty students over a period of time, offering them different courses according to their skills. Some taught as many as 800 students at different times. The homes of these women and others with specific skills became community homes, mainly for girls and women, but also for boys, and were financed and managed entirely by women. Women and girls spread the news about the secret schools to their peers by word of mouth. They hid their books, notebooks, pens and pencils under their *burqas*, and risked their lives by going to the secret schools every day. Here they not only received basic literacy and numeracy training, but also studied different subjects at various levels, such as biology, chemistry, engineering, English, German, Arabic, Qur'anic studies, cooking, sewing, knitting and hairdressing.

Education was, therefore, at the heart of women's struggle. Orzala Ashraf was twenty-two when she established Humanitarian Assistance for the Women and Children of Afghanistan (HAWCA) in Pakistan and later in Afghanistan. She described her feelings:

> As a little girl I used to go and visit my uncles in jail under the communist government. They were not allowed pen and papers. I used to smuggle pen and papers for them under my clothes. They were all killed either by the Soviet invaders or the Mujaheddin. To be able to cope with such a great loss, I decided to help the younger generation by teaching them in the refugee camps.

Kabul was conquered by the Taliban in 1996. Kabul University's female professors went to Bamiyan and set up a university there until Bamiyan too fell to the Taliban forces in 1998. Humera Rahi taught Persian literature at the University of Bamiyan. She emerged as a leading poet of resistance among the Hazaras, who suffered brutal oppression.[23] Suraya Paikan established the Afghan Women Lawyers and Professional Association in 1998 in Mazar-e-Sharif. The organization had 400 active members. They were forced to leave Afghanistan by the Taliban but they continued their work in Peshawar and in 2001 they returned to Kabul. Those with the necessary skills turned their homes into underground schools. They were paid for these services by their neighbours, friends and family. In this way, they were able to survive financially. Ghamar's husband was killed in the civil war. She had a daughter. She secretly taught more than 800 students in her home. Women in the neighbourhood paid her as much as they could to teach their children; without her, their daughters would have been illiterate. Shukria, who won a seat in the parliamentary elections in 2005, worked secretly under the Taliban. She described the impact of her organization: 'We were twenty-three women working as teachers. We taught 650 students [who] did not know about our NGO ... [But] I am proud today that they have realized that their secret lessons were organized by our NGO.'

The UN organizations and the Taliban agreed on certain projects to distribute food and other aid such as baking bread and making soup. Throughout the rule of the Taliban, women took these opportunities to teach secretly, and even managed to distribute printed materials for their secret education. Although ethnic conflict was at its highest level during the Mujaheddin and the Taliban, women of diverse groups (Shi'a, Sunni, Pashtun, Tajik, Uzbek) worked together on these food projects and in their secret schools. For example, Farzana pointed out that:

> Despite many problems, we had ten different cultural societies for young women in ten different parts of Mazar-e-Sharif. It was a very active time for young women. We cooked food and

> went door to door to distribute food and under the pretext of giving food to them, we discussed with them about freedom and democracy. Of course, because most women were illiterate, we tried to discuss these issues with them in the form of storytelling.

Many women involved in education were caught by the Taliban. But even though they were persecuted, jailed and tortured, they continued their bitter struggle. The Taliban's intelligence agency was an extension of the agency that had operated during the communist regime. They employed between 15,000 and 30,000 professional spies as well as having 100,000 paid informers.[24] Some of these spies and informers were women. There are no statistics about women who were actively engaged with the Taliban, but the numbers were greater in the Pashtun provinces than in other provinces. The Taliban mobilized their women supporters to suppress the anti-Taliban women and their activities. In most cases women cooperated with male Taliban because of poverty, famine and hunger. But there were some women who agreed with their menfolk and it was in their material and ideological interest to support violence and conflict. They exercised agency by ruthlessly suppressing the anti-Taliban women. With the approval of the Taliban, they were in charge of those UN and NGO projects that distributed food and other vital resources. Rahima explained:

> Many times I was punished for organizing classes for women. Once I was prosecuted by a group of Taliban women. They argued that women are the weak sex and should remain at home and perform their domestic duties. They accused me of acting against the philosophy of Prophet Muhammad for involving women in social activities. I challenged them and argued against them. I said to them, women are not the weak sex, their activities outside the home are not against the philosophy of Prophet Muhammad and they themselves are a good example of this.

After the fall of the Taliban, these women, like their menfolk, opportunistically changed their positions and worked with the new system. Some have now reached positions of power and decision-making. Others led a quiet life and some still believe in Taliban ideology but don't express their views publicly for fear of persecution. Halima said:

> Aisha, who lives in the neighbourhood, was one of the pro-Taliban women, now she has taken off her *chaddari* and says that she never was a Taliban. During the famine, the Taliban agreed that we cook and distribute food. Aisha had an official letter to enter our houses to check on us. She followed us everywhere and if she did not agree with what we did she reported us to be punished. She did not even pray. We asked her why she was missing her prayers. She said if I pray you may do things behind my back which could be against the Taliban's custom.

Women's mobility depended entirely on *burqa* and *mahram*. Many women used these strategies to continue their secret activities; many men bravely accompanied women to their secret schools and organizations and some were punished, arrested, tortured or killed for supporting women. Sometimes it was not possible to have a *mahram*, for example if there was no man in the family: a woman had to get married to have a *mahram*. Sometimes the Taliban would force women to get married just for this reason. However, some women bravely and imaginatively came up with the idea of hiring a *mahram*. Sima explained:

> We paid a man from within the extended family or neighbourhood to pretend that he is our *mahram* and to accompany us in public so that we could go to work. This was also one way for these men to have a job and earn money. In these cases, women's secret work allowed men to earn money. But it was risky for both men and women because if the Taliban would have found out we would have been dead.

In order to understand the gendered nature of Afghan men's experiences of subordination, I asked a number of men whether this was against their masculine identity and if they felt it was a loss of face to be hired by women in order to earn money. Shikeb explained: 'No, for us this was a way of supporting our women, family and community. This was not against our masculine identity. We felt loss of respect and insult to our masculine identity when we were humiliated in public during the civil war and Taliban by other men.'

Women today feel that, under the Taliban, women and men were closer to each other and were more motivated to work for their communities than under the US-led invasion. Feriba said: 'In a strange way we miss that period. For days we didn't go home to do our domestic chores because we were involved in struggle against the Taliban. In a strange way, it was an exciting time. We were doing everything wholeheartedly, we had no good shoes and clothes, but what we did was extremely rewarding.'

Under the Taliban rule, women's activities were concentrated on the provision of secret schools and survival. After the fall of the Taliban they began to challenge patriarchal gender relations as well as challenging the western perception of Muslim women, especially the view about the wearing of *burqa*. Farida commented angrily: 'All I hear since the fall of Taliban is *chaddari, chaddari, chaddari*. My problem is not *chaddari*; my problem is that I don't have any food to feed myself and my children.' Nasira agreed:

> The Taliban imposed it on us. After five years ... [it has] become part of our culture, we feel comfortable with it. Our community and society do not accept women without *chaddari*. We will not take it off just because the West wants us to ... Some of us may take it off once we are ready and our society is ready. To be pressured by the West to take off our *chaddari* is as bad as Taliban imposing [it] on us [in the first place]. We have the right to choose what to wear.[25]

Women in Afghanistan have experienced twenty-two years of war, civil war and violent conflict. Sima Wali,[26] who became Minister for Women after the fall of the Taliban, argued that most Afghans rejected the popular perception that the crimes committed in Afghanistan over those years could be attributed to the growth of extremist Islam and tribalism. She felt that Afghanistan was betrayed by the world, especially by the United States which used Afghanistan as a tool in the battle against the Soviet Union and, once its objectives were met, ignored the needs of the Afghan people.

Despite this, women have bravely sought out alternative ways of surviving and formulating their objectives within the context of restricted resources and cultural practices. There can be no doubt that these years have eroded social capital in Afghanistan. However, under the most adverse conditions of the Taliban regime, Afghan women and men relied upon social relations and mutual support. This was the most important asset through which they kept their families and communities together and it enabled them to survive the Taliban regime. They built the foundation for creating social capital which was essential for the process of reconstruction. Women worked together in groups and organizations, generating networks, norms and trust in their communities. They helped each other and the most vulnerable women through their secret schools. They consolidated their role as social actors and they had great hopes that after the fall of the Taliban their situation would improve and they could aim at broadening democracy in their society.

Notes

1 Dupree 1984: 313.

2 There is a debate about the use of the term 'warlords'. Warlords do not constitute a homogeneous group; some were/are more powerful than others and performed/perform different functions. Not all warlords are unpopular; election results demonstrated that people such as Dostum and Mohaqiq had popular support. See Sedra 2002; and Giustozzi 2003 and 2004. I am grateful to Jonathan Goodhand and Alessandro Monsutti for bringing this to my attention.

3 It has been argued that she

was assassinated by Hekmatyar's associates. See Brodsky 2003: 91–2.

4 Shahrani 1984: 66.

5 Dupree 1998.

6 Ibid.

7 Ibid.

8 Tapper 1984; and Dupree 1984.

9 Rubin 2002: 17; Pain and Goodhand 2002: 22.

10 Quoted in Callinicos 2003: 10; and Ali 2002: 208–9.

11 Barakat and Wardell 2001: 16.

12 Rashid 2001: 128–42.

13 Rashid 2000: 18, 23.

14 Barakat and Wardell 2001.

15 Rashid 2000: 110; and Afghanland 2005.

16 Pain and Goodhand 2002.

17 Barakat and Wardell 2001.

18 Quoted in Rashid 2000: 217–18.

19 Johnson and Leslie 2004: 83.

20 Rubin 2002.

21 Rostami-Povey 2004a and 2004b.

22 For this discussion see Moser and Clark 2001.

23 Rashid 2000: 68–9.

24 Ibid.: 106.

25 Rostami-Povey 2004a and 2004b.

26 In 2002, she became Minister for Women's Affairs but was forced out of her job for objecting to the continued role of warlords in the government. See Chapter 3.

3 | Under invasion

> 'We hate them when in the name of women's rights and human rights they come and intrude on our privacy. They keep saying women should work. They don't understand that women are not happy that they provide work for women and not for men. It does not work like this in our culture. We want to work side by side with our men. We cannot ignore our men. Men also need education and employment.' Nuria, Mazar-e-Sharif

In October 2001 the administration in Washington, supported by the UK government, led a bombing campaign against Afghanistan. American and British forces began an aerial bombardment, targeting Taliban and al-Qaida forces in Kabul, Kandahar, Konduz, Herat and Jalalabad. In November 2001, the US bombers carpet-bombed Mazar-e-Sharif. In many instances, the bombs fell on villages and urban residential areas, which were already damaged from the long years of war. An estimated 400 civilians were killed in the first week of bombing. The number of dead reached an estimated 4,000 in the following three months, many more houses were destroyed, animals were killed[1] and 2.2 million people were internally displaced. Bombs were dropped on fleeing refugees, the majority of them women and children. Ambulances carrying injured refugees were also attacked. UN mine-clearing officials noted that 14,000 unexploded cluster bombs killed and maimed between 40 and 100 people a week. The bombing campaign broke down the already fragile infrastructure of aid distribution which had existed under the Taliban. UN and international relief agencies warned of the catastrophic consequences of the bombing campaign as hundreds of thousands were on the brink of starvation. In response, George W. Bush stated that at the same time as they were targeting Taliban and al-Qaida, food and medical supplies would be dropped to the starving people of Afghanistan.[2]

The purpose of the bombing campaign was to oust al-Qaida members and their leader Osama Bin Laden and to punish the Taliban government for supporting al-Qaida. By mid-November, the Taliban and al-Qaida had regrouped their forces in the mountains of Tora Bora near Pakistan's border. The US air strike on Tora Bora led to the defeat of Taliban and al-Qaida forces. However, Osama Bin Laden and important al-Qaida figures escaped to the tribal border areas between Afghanistan and Pakistan. They soon regained their strength and began launching cross-border raids on US/NATO forces. Taliban forces also regained their strength in the rural regions of the four southern provinces of Kandahar, Zabul, Helmand and Uruzgan. These insurgents used the region as a base for launching attacks on the invading forces.[3]

With the fall of the Taliban, Afghan women expected much from the process of reconstruction. By 2007, any optimism that Afghanistan might have been entering a new era of peace, security and development had been swept away. The United Nations Development Programme (UNDP) and the World Bank[4] argue that reconstruction and development are urgently needed, otherwise the country is likely to slip back into chaos and abject poverty. Thirty-nine per cent of the population in urban areas and 69 per cent in rural areas do not have access to clean water. One in eight children dies because of contaminated water; life expectancy is forty-four years; 53 per cent of the total population live below the poverty line; the adult literacy rate is 29 per cent and in some areas less than 1 per cent of the population is literate. Only a few sub-Saharan nations rank lower than Afghanistan. Very little has been invested in reconstruction. Out of 21,000 kilometres of roads, only 2,793 kilometres are paved. There are forty-seven airports, but only ten have paved runways.[5]

Women are victims of a state that has directed its attention towards militarization rather than housing, health, education, infrastructure and welfare. Three hundred families in Bamiyan live in the caves in absolute poverty at the sides of a famous ancient Buddha that was destroyed by the Taliban.[6] In Kabul, where the US-led invaders are partially in control, a five-star hotel, the first escalator and a shopping centre with coffee-bars have been built. The shopping centre displays Apple iPods, the latest mobile phones and giant flat-screen televisions for the western and Japanese contractors, the international community and a few privileged Afghan customers. Outside the shopping centre, open sewers run through the streets. Day labourers stand from dawn to dusk hoping for a day's work, but none comes, and women queue to be handed a piece of bread by NGOs.[7] There is no economic policy to intervene and provide opportunities for people to participate in the market economy, no policy to allow for the distribution of benefits.[8] After nearly six years, the International Security Assistance Force (ISAF), USA and NATO forces and their client state have failed to bring about economic development, peace and security. The term 'Iraqification' has been used to describe the neglect of reconstruction in Afghanistan and the increase in suicide bombing.[9]

A rentier state has been propped up by foreign aid and opium revenue, with no engagement with society. The majority of the population live in absolute poverty and despair while watching a tiny minority grow wealthy with the help of international financial organizations. According to the UN High Commissioner for Refugees (UNHCR), 4 million people in Afghanistan are dependent on aid. The growing conflict in the south of the country has obstructed the delivery of aid and, as in previous years, hundreds of thousands are dying of starvation.[10] Poverty has led to massive corruption. Nothing can be done without paying the 'middle man'. Being a 'middle man' is a job and a way to survive. Damaged buildings are not demolished and rebuilt; in some cases, two or three floors are built on top of damaged foundations. As a result, buildings have collapsed, killing many people.[11] Even NATO secretary general Jaap de Hoop Scheffer said, in October 2006, that 'there is no military solution for Afghanistan'.[12]

Security has worsened. UK spending on the 'war on terror' is £2 million a day and US spending is approximately $35 billion per year.[13] According to the UN's security assessment for Afghanistan, half of the country is categorized as either extreme risk or high risk and the other half is categorized as medium to low risk.[14] Al-Qaida is recruiting Arabs and Chechens, Pashtuns and Uzbeks and providing them with weapons and bomb-making devices. Local warlords and commanders such as Gulbuddin Hekmatyar, a CIA favourite in the 1980s, have now become the enemy of the USA, equipping gunmen with technologically advanced weapons and roadside bombs. He is not the only one; other warlords and commanders who have turned against the invading forces pay unemployed young men up to £2,600 for planting roadside bombs to kill foreign invaders.[15] As in the civil war and the Taliban period, the *madrassas* in Peshawar are once again the recruiting centres. In response, NATO is using air strikes against them, killing thousands of civilians. Out of this chaos, al-Qaida and the Taliban are winning the hearts and minds of the local population. Chris Johnson and Jolyon Leslie argue that when the Taliban came to power, they brought security and allowed the distribution of humanitarian aid; now under US, ISAF and NATO forces, Afghanistan is gradually moving backwards to how it was during the civil war.[16] Women's demands for food security, clean water, refugee issues and an end to trafficking have fallen on deaf ears.

The reality is that the US-led invasion of Afghanistan in 2001 was not about peace, security and development or women's liberation and democracy. The western hegemonic alliance rationalized a system of governance in Afghanistan to facilitate the West's desire to control Central Asia in the face of the potential danger of pressure from Russia, China and India for autonomous development.[17] The plan for the control of

Central Asia and the Middle East did not start with the war in Afghanistan. Its root is in the failure of neo-liberalism and the emergence of neo-conservatism. Throughout the 1980s and 1990s, African, Asian and Latin American countries were driven to adopt neo-liberalism (a free market economy, privatization and shrinking the role of the state) and open their markets to the transnational corporations (TNCs). The claim was that industrialized countries provide resources and opportunities to developing countries and these countries should take advantage of these opportunities. However, the needs of developing countries were disregarded as the powerful industrialized countries, according to their own interests, decided which resources and opportunities should be provided and ignored what developing countries needed. The end of the 1990s revealed the failure of neo-liberalism to bring about prosperity in developing countries.[18]

In the USA, neo-conservatism was seen as the answer to the failure of neo-liberalism. The election of George W. Bush brought to power neo-conservative thinkers who believed that to achieve the end of US global economic domination, neo-liberalism could, and should, be imposed on the whole world through military intervention. David Harvey argues that neo-conservatism is consistent with the neo-liberal agenda of 'elite governance, mistrust of democracy, and the maintenance of market freedoms', but that it has reshaped neo-liberal practices in two fundamental respects: 'first in its concern for *order* as an answer to the chaos of individual interests, and second, in its concern for an overweening *morality* as the necessary social glue to keep the body politic secure in the face of external and internal dangers'.[19] The National Security Strategy (NSS) of the USA clearly states that it is committed to spreading the US model of capitalism and democracy throughout the world, by military means if necessary. Under US domination, countries around the globe are allowed to develop economically providing they are loyal to the ideology of neo-liberalism and neo-conservatism.[20] Under this regime of American hegemony, the powers of governments in developing countries are limited. Individualism and private property are protected. Democracy is not about voting and popular sovereignty but about the institutions that allow this American model to flourish. Those governments and countries that are not prepared to be subordinated will face restrictions and will be excluded from the global economy.[21]

Against this background George Bush, supported by Tony Blair, invaded Afghanistan. The war against the Taliban was justified as self-defence in response to terrorist acts in the USA. The UN Security Council recognized the right to self-defence in accordance with the UN charter, but did not explicitly authorize the use of force.[22] The events of 9/11 were the motivating force for the invasion of Afghanistan. The rise of neo-conservatism and 9/11 speeded up the desire to control Central Asia and the Middle East. In the USA, neo-conservatism, backed by Christian fundamentalism, the military–industrial complex and Zionism, turned the warfare waged for the extension of neo-liberalism around the globe into aggressive confrontation. The NSS states that, after the war in Afghanistan, the establishment of US military bases and deployment of US forces in Central Asia and the Middle East became a priority. Washington adopted a policy of 'security and development' in Afghanistan.[23] Within this framework, according to global liberal governance, state and non-state actors (governments, international NGOs, the military, private companies, UN organizations and international financial institutions) were brought together to free Afghanistan from the threat of terrorism, rebuilding the war-torn society in order to achieve development, stability, women's liberation and democracy, all in the context of a free market economy.[24]

Many international organizations, including the World Bank, the International Monetary Fund (IMF), the World Trade Organization (WTO), UN organizations and international NGOs operate in Afghanistan. There are also foreign embassies and the ISAF and NATO forces. These are under heavy armed protection and are situated in the central Kabul and a few other urban cities. To the resentment of the local population, these organizations, foreign contractors and a few rich Afghans, buy diesel generators for electricity while the majority, even in Kabul, have no electricity or clean water. Poor families struggle to meet the costs of water and fuel. These factors, together with overcrowded and unhygienic living conditions, are the cause of many deaths.[25]

Poverty and years of war, violent conflicts and displacement can lead to three generations living under one roof. People feel a great need to support each other after so many years of separation and displacement. Yet such overcrowding means that young people in particular suffer from lack of space and privacy. No one dares to be out in the streets after sunset. Drugs, violence and the abduction of children and young women are widespread. Moreover, there is the danger of being shot by security forces or run over by their fast cars patrolling the streets.

The investment that could have increased demand for female labour has not been made and women's unemployment continues to be abysmally high. Limited levels of skills and low demand for female labour lock women into a restricted range of income-generating activities, mainly in agriculture and handicrafts. In Kabul and a few other urban areas, a small number of women work for international NGOs, UN organizations, foreign embassies and ISAF. These organizations pay a higher wage than Afghan's state and private institutions. However, little has been done for the majority of women. Rural poverty, landlessness and homelessness have resulted in a mass rural-to-urban labour migration. Despite continuing social restriction on women, a large number of internal migrants are women, but conditions of work for women in urban areas are more exploitative than for men.[26]

Urban labour markets are diversified, but for the majority who constitute the unskilled and illiterate labour force, opportunities for men are limited to daily and casual labour such as construction work, pulling carts and running mobile shops in wheelbarrows. As in the Taliban period, a large number of women are engaged in begging and sex work. Some women work as servants and carpet weavers. For many families, young girls are treated like a commodity and are valued for the money they may bring in as a bride price.

International security forces

According to international law and the Geneva Convention, occupying forces have to assist civil populations and to provide them with basic services. On this basis, there is an assumption that the presence of international security forces in Afghanistan is positive, because international organizations and NGOs feel safe to work in order to create jobs and security for the population, especially for women and girls. In reality, though, the majority of the population hates the Provisional Reconstruction Teams (PRTs) – a mixture of soldiers and civilian aid workers. PRTs have come to mean that soldiers shoot and kill people in the morning and aid workers distribute aid in the evening.[27] Mirwaiz in Mazar-e-Sharif said, 'We hate them when they come with their guns and claim that they have come to repair our houses and schools.' A woman whose blind husband was dragged from their home as an al-Qaida suspect, cursed the Americans 'as *kafar* [the infidels] who raided her home, disrespected her religion and culture and created misery and fear for her and the neighbourhood'. According to communal gender relations based on the Afghan code of honour, an Afghan man must protect and care for his wife and his family. The provision of work for women by foreign invading forces is threatening to both women's and men's cultural identity, in particular to men's masculine identity as the breadwinners. Under these circumstances, women sided with their men. They demanded employment opportunities to be created for both men and women. Feriba in Mazar-e-Sharif argued:

> Women, especially, hate the PRT because in the name of women's rights and human rights they come and intrude on our privacy. They keep saying women should work. They don't understand that women are not happy when they provide some work for women but not for men. It does not work like this in our culture. We want to work side by side with our men. We cannot ignore our men. Men also need education, employment and training.

In different parts of the country, foreign contractors are building massive walls around large areas, which their own Afghan workers are not allowed to enter. The Afghan government, parliament and media do not object to or even discuss this issue. People in these areas feel that they have been kept in the dark by their own institutions. They believe that the contractors are building military installations and camps and/or stealing Afghanistan resources. Najia explained: 'My husband works for them. He and his friends fill the lorry with sand and earth and drive the lorry to the area near the walls and empty them all day long. They are not allowed to go inside the work area. They pay in dollars, so even those people who hate them work for them. They have no choice if they want to feed their families.'

Men feel keenly the loss of respect when they are dragged out of their homes and beaten up by foreign troops as suspected members of the Taliban and al-Qaida. Haroon commented: 'This reminds us of the days that we were humiliated in public during the civil war and Taliban by other men in charge. We also resent being treated in a patronizing way by the UN or international NGOs who, anyway, ignore men's needs.' Women in particular are concerned about security. With the exception of Kabul city centre, women do not go out of the house or travel without wearing the *burqa* and without being accompanied by their husbands or male blood relatives. These conventions were forced on them by the Taliban, ostensibly to protect them from being raped and murdered by rival groups. Under the US-led invasion, women have had no choice but to continue these practices because they do not feel safe.

Halima, a women's rights activist from Jalalabad, argued that women do not take the *burqa* off because, 'there is no security. We don't trust many people around us. Some of the men who are part of the security system and working with the US-led invaders were Mujaheddin and then became Taliban and now they are security officers. We don't want to be exposed to them as women's rights activists.'

Security forces kick, swear at and beat up people in the streets. They terrorize people when traffic jams are created by the large numbers of UN, NGO and the ISAF vehicles filling city centres. The word 'motherfucker' is used so often that many Afghan men use this terminology for the foreigners – they may not know the meaning of the word but they know it is derogatory.

Security problems have worsened significantly since mid-2004. Civilians have become caught in the crossfire of a vicious rural war. The southern provinces of Helmand, Kandahar and Nangarhar, the so-called 'Pashto Belt' (dominated by Pashto-speaking ethnic groups), are shifting from a limited state control to control by the Taliban groups which use political violence and the opium economy to strengthen their power base. They are also advancing to the eastern provinces, and the Bush administration's dependence on cooperation between Pakistan and Afghanistan to fight against Taliban advances is diminishing rapidly. The Afghanistan Insurgency Assessment has argued that the Pakistanization of southern Afghanistan is on the way economically, socially and politically. The Afghan currency has no value. Trade, mainly in opium and heroin, takes place in Pakistani rupees and there is a sharp rise in intermarriage between the Pakistani and Afghan Pashtuns.[28] This is a significant development. As mentioned earlier, historically there have been few marriages between Pakistanis and

Afghans, so this trend seems to indicate a cementing of ties with Pakistan against the Afghan government. Sharp inequalities, the corruption of state officials and the total failure to control the opium economy has increased anti-foreign demonstrations and violence. The vast majority of people are increasingly angry about the failure of the government and the invaders to bring about peace, security and development.[29] In this new world of unrest, violence and insecurity, the terms post-conflict and post-Taliban have become meaningless.

The UN and international NGOs

The impact of UN agencies and international NGOs has been localized and small-scale. They are the weakest link in the chain of state and non-state cooperation and are unable to do any meaningful reconstruction. The economically and militaristically powerful states and governments exercise their power through these organizations and shape the economic policy of Afghanistan. In their policy statements, we note that the influence of the neo-conservative and neo-liberal logic of 'security and development' is pervasive. It is on these terms that the military and NGOs interact. Many NGOs and UN organizations are not comfortable with such an alliance. The phenomenon of 'security and development' makes it difficult for them to separate their traditional non-governmental and humanitarian activities from the dominant imperialist agenda supported by politically and militaristically powerful governments.[30] Private companies and international NGOs under the protection of the military are increasingly taking over the provision of health, education and other public goods and services. Such services can provide a degree of health, education and other benefits at local levels but they do not reach the majority of the population.

Afghan women working for these organizations feel that even their languages are under threat. Considering the level of illiteracy, they find the use of English-language terminology by

NGOs, the UN organizations, as well as television programmes and the internet, oppressive. Terms such as 'gender', 'development', 'participatory rural appraisal', 'democracy' and 'planning', are now used by illiterate or partially educated women and men who work with UN and NGO projects. They do not understand the real meaning of these terms and cannot find their Dari or Pashto equivalents. Many are questioning whether these organizations, with all their good intentions, are contributing to the improvement of people's life in Afghanistan or unwittingly cooperating in the twenty-first-century US-dominated imperial reconstruction. They also feel that their culture is under threat, as many projects on gender, human rights and democracy are based on the western culture of individuality and fail to understand Afghan women's relations to their family and community. Najia in Jalalabad said:

> There are so many international organizations, some are trying their best, but they are miles away from understanding our situation and our culture. They keep talking about women's rights and democracy. People are hungry and sick. I work with ordinary women and men and try to explain to them that Islam has given rights to women. This is the only way to fight for women's rights in Afghanistan, to show to women and men the positive side of Islam and Islamic culture, not from outside, and not by insulting people's culture and religion.

Fouzia, who has returned to Afghanistan from the USA, and Nargis, who has returned from the UK to participate in the reconstruction of their country feel alienated and unable to do anything. They said:

> We are strangers here. We are a part of the small elite group that has returned from the West. On the one hand, we are snubbed by the representatives of the western institutions who are running the country and on the other hand we do not fit with the Afghan society and the people on the ground. We have our

> own gatherings and are detached from ordinary people. I am supposed to be working on human rights issues and women's issues but ordinary people keep their distance from me. This is painful. It was not a choice for me to leave Afghanistan and now that I have made a choice to return, I am being rejected by my own people. I feel that there is not much I can do here.

Everywhere women feel disappointed and angry. Bibisafia said: 'In reality the money which comes into Afghanistan from one door goes out from another door, because Afghans are not being absorbed into the NGOs and UN organizations.' Tajbanoo similarly argued that:

> Their aim was not liberating Afghanistan; their aim was to steal our resources. Afghanistan has now become a workplace for foreign specialists either through western governments or international organizations. They employ American, European and Japanese doctors and engineers and pay them large amounts of money to work in Afghanistan. Why they don't employ Afghan specialists? We have doctors and engineers and all kinds of specialists, even if there are shortages of Afghan specialists; why don't they employ us and train us? They are not helping us, they are helping themselves. They have ruined our country and now they have invaded our country in the name of reconstruction. I hope that history will show the truth one day.

Shahbibi Shah described how shocked she was when she went from London to Kabul:

> Before I went to Kabul, whenever people criticized the NGOs and the UN organizations I got angry and I thought how mean people are to criticize these organizations who are trying to help people in Afghanistan. When I went to Kabul, I realized that all the criticisms that I heard were valid. I was shocked to see the level of poverty and despair and no one to help these poor people. I came to the conclusion that they are obviously there as part of the big imperial agenda.

Local NGOs such as the Afghan Women Network (AWN), the Afghan Women Council (AWC), Humanitarian Assistance for the Women and Children of Afghanistan (HAWCA) and the Revolutionary Association of the Women of Afghanistan (RAWA), among others, which provided health and education to Afghan refugee women in Pakistan, are now engaged in health, education and the provision of shelter for women and children in different parts of Afghanistan. Their role in Pakistan and in Afghanistan is crucial. Without them, the level of poverty, ill-health, illiteracy and women's desperate situation would almost certainly be even worse than it already is. However, as is argued by Johnson and Leslie, the days when NGOs and UN organizations performed their humanitarian responsibilities independently of governments and international financial institutions which are committed to the free market economy have passed. Furthermore, the lack of any meaningful reconstruction and the continuing presence of foreign troops have created resentment and hostility.

The state, foreign private companies and the warlords

Reconstruction in Afghanistan is driven by the private sector and organized within the free market. In the absence of Afghan entrepreneurs, the limited reconstruction that does take place involves foreign companies, commanders and warlords, facilitated by the state. For most women, however, the most important issue was genuine economic reconstruction and the integration of all ethnic groups into development programmes. Women see their right to housing as a basic human right, being ignored by the alliance of commanders, warlords, the state and their foreign allies. They resent the big houses and businesses which are being built by foreign contractors, the commanders and warlords.[31] As Adela stated:

> It is painful for us to see that the same commanders and warlords who committed crimes such as rape, murder and

> forced us out of our land, our home and our property are now in power. We demand from this government to distribute the lands, homes, properties to the rightful owners. Those who have come back from exile have no home to go back to and have to pay high rents. Many escaped the terror and violence of Mujaheddin and Taliban and they did not take their documents with them. Today they cannot prove that the land, the home, the building are theirs. Even those who have something to prove, they don't have the power and opportunity to fight for their rights.

The promotion of private sector growth has provided an opening for warlords and commanders. Through privatization of resources they are in control of most businesses to varying degrees. Some have made alliances with each other and some have not. Besides economic power, each group has different levels of local political power.[32] Large and small private companies as well as TNCs are operating to exploit the resources of Afghanistan. Afghans are concerned about the future of their economy being based on partnership between foreign and warlords' capital.

UN and international NGO workers are not allowed to travel with Afghan airlines because they are not safe. No investment has been made to make Afghan airlines safe to travel with. Instead, a number of western private airline companies provide services for foreign workers under the name of 'provision of services for Humanitarian, Relief and Development Projects and Organizations'. They charge between US$60 and $1,600 per destination depending on the distance and the security situation of the area. In the eyes of the Afghans, 'the invading forces are not reconstructing, they are making huge amounts of profit out of Afghanistan's destruction'.

The alliance with the warlords and commanders is a part of the strategy of US-led invasion to shift the balance of power between different groups so that the past problems of ethnic conflicts do not arise. This is considered as a good move, based on the belief that they have changed their positions and have been reformed. However, these groups are working with the government, on the one hand, and, on the other hand, working with anti-government groups in other parts of Afghanistan. They all have their own armed privatized security forces and resist state authority. Political parties approved by the government have continued their alliance with the warlords and their military factions and are in conflict with local government officials.

In the eyes of the majority of the population, the political actors, whether in the parliament or the government, lack legitimacy. The UN and the USA invested a massive amount of money and other resources in the presidential election in 2004 and the parliamentary election in 2005. However, in the absence of socio-economic development and security, elections are meaningless. The constitutional process consolidated the position of the Pashtuns in the government. They are out of touch with the majority of the population, including the grassroots Pashtuns. The Pashtun dominance in the government runs the risk of deepening ethnic divisions within the country. The powerful warlords and commanders who are part of the government and the parliament continue to fight each other. The UN, NGOs and Human Rights Watch, working on gender issues, constantly report that they face hostility and their work has been undermined by the conflict between local government institutions and political parties.[33]

The opium economy

The resurgent opium economy props up the new government's fragile hold on Afghanistan. Opium is crucial to the power of the warlords on whom foreign troops and the Afghan regime depend. Outside Kabul, the country is in the control of a federation of local rulers, commanders and warlords, all reinforced by drug profits. Opium production, export and profit in Afghanistan are similar to oil production, export and profit in the Middle East. In 2004, opium cultivation increased by as much as 64 per cent, pouring $2.8 billion in illicit revenue into the pockets of warlords and traffickers.[34] In 2000, 82,000 hectares were under cultivation. In 2001, under the Taliban, this was reduced to 8,000 hectares. In contrast, since the fall of the Taliban, the area under opium cultivation has increased to 74,000 in 2002, 80,000 in 2003 and 131,000 in 2004. It was reduced to 104,000 in 2005, but it increased to 165,000 hectares in 2006.[35]

If there was a genuine economic policy to help Afghan people, investment in the agricultural sector could have become a viable alternative to the opium economy. But there is no incentive for internal or international investment in rural infrastructure. International organizations and western governments sometimes wage a military anti-drug campaign (burning poppy fields in some parts in order to wipe them out) and sometimes rhetorically promise alternative economic opportunities combined with law enforcement. However, no real attempt has been made to invest in agriculture, industry or services. For the majority of people, the only available option to achieve food security is to be engaged in the poppy economy. Hamida discussed how for some this is a question of survival and for others a means of making massive profits:

> The price of opium changes from one hand to another hand. Some are better quality and some are mixed with fruit and are cheaper. For the poor women and men who work on the land, it is just survival. For the traffickers and people on top, it is huge profit. In some areas producers are not addicted, they even feel guilty that it will fall into the hands of those who may abuse it and use it for heroin and addiction.

Aga Khan Development Network's report about Badakhshan, the extreme north-eastern province, argues that some areas are consumption areas and some areas are production areas. In the consumption areas, a large number of the population are addicted. Consumption is high and people use opium to fight unbearable amounts of sickness and pain caused by years of poor nutrition, sleeping in cold conditions and constant cycles of pregnancy in women. According to this report, pregnant women addicts either deliver stillborn babies or give birth to addicted babies. When they breastfeed, the babies' addiction grows. Opium consumption is relatively lower among families with higher standards of living and is higher among poorer households. They give opium to their children to curb their hunger, to keep them quiet and calm and in times of sickness. Older children cannot go to school without a dose of opium. Accidental death from an overdose is common among children. Widespread opium addiction is often the source of conflict between husbands and wives. When men are addicted they cannot provide adequately for their families, and when women are addicted they face disapproval from their husbands. Both cases lead to violence against women. In many cases, male opium addicts who become impotent force their wives to become addicts, with the aim of reducing the incidence of infidelity. These experiences are not specific to Badakhshan province. For the majority of the population, opium, in one form or another, simply equates with survival. Poverty and the absence of healthcare have led to vicious circles of consumption and addiction.[36]

Commanders, warlords and drug traffickers force people to work on their land through intimidation and keep farmers in debt. People sell or mortgage their land and they sell their household belongings to pay for their debt plus interest. In other cases, families send their young girls and boys to work in the fields of traders in the form of bonded labour. Selling young girls or marrying them off to richer, older men in return for money which could be used to repay debts is widespread. Despite unprecedented high prices for opium, they succeed in paying only a section of their debt and systematically fail to regain their land.[37]

Shari'a law gives women the right to own property. Years of conflict, however, have meant that, in practice, this is relatively rare. However, the widows and female-headed households, whose numbers are high[38] (no reliable statistics are available), have gained limited rights over the land. They are not permitted to sell the land, only to pass it to their male kin. Some work on the land themselves and others give the land to other farmers to work for a share of the crop. Landless and poorer women work on land as wage workers. Rural poverty has also changed the traditional divisions of labour (see Chapter 1). In households where there is no male kin, women work from sewing to harvesting to processing. Women are also engaged in non-farm labour, carpet weaving, sewing, embroidery, jewellery and hat making. The drought has made families more dependent on income from carpet weaving. In some cases, female-headed households with access to cash employ male workers in exchange for feeding them. Unlike other women, widows buy the necessary goods and sell the finished goods themselves. Nevertheless, they cannot survive on any of these kinds of work. Instead they become engaged in opium production. Women actively participate in the various stages of opium cultivation and their labour has become crucial because of the intensive manual work required during the six-month growing cycle.[39] Nargis explained: 'they cannot survive if they produce fruit, vegetables or weave carpets. They earn more money this way. For example, it is impossible to have access to electricity and water, but some of those who are producing opium are able to buy electricity and water.'

All these cases demonstrate that poverty and years of war have led to change in traditional gender relations and divisions of labour. In the absence of men, female-headed households can have access to land and cash income. They can also have the power of decision-making. However, absolute poverty makes a change in gender relations meaningless. If agriculture becomes a viable alternative to the opium economy, these changes may improve women's situation as their contribution to the economy has historically been important. Opium cultivation cannot offer sustainable solutions to women's economic needs or their gender rights. They remain vulnerable, voiceless and powerless.

Women and reconstruction

In December 2001, 200 women participated in the 1,550-member Loya Jirga, the traditional grand assembly. Mahbuba Hoquqmal, a lawyer, was one of the twenty-one people chosen by the United Nations out of 1,000 to decide how the Loya Jirga should convene and how the transitional government should be formed. Three women delegates (Sima Wali, Sima Samar and Suhaila Seddiqi) participated in the UN-sponsored Bonn negotiations to form an Afghan interim government. They demanded the creation of a Ministry of Women's Affairs and the appointment of Sima Samar as the Minister of Women's Affairs and Suhaila Seddiqi as the Minister for Public Health. However, Sima Samar was forced out of her job for objecting to the continued role of warlords and commanders in the government confirmed by the Loya Jirga.[40] Habiba Sarabi replaced Sima Samar, but she was forced to dismiss 150 of her female staff.[41] Through pressure from women activists, Sima Samar became the director of the Human Rights Commission. Habiba Sarabi was appointed as governor of Bamiyan province. Mahbuba Hoquqmal became the State Minister for Women. At the constitutional Loya Jirga in December 2003, 25 per cent of the delegates were women.

These organizations, together with international NGOs, UN organizations and international financial institutions, became involved in integrating gender equality into policies, programmes and projects supposedly enabling women to participate in decision-making. However, despite these positive gestures, no attention is paid to women's material well-being. The erosion of livelihoods, growing poverty, the opium economy and insecurity make the constitutional and formal rights meaningless. The constitution guarantees women's equal rights with men. Afghanistan has joined various UN conventions on women's rights and human rights such as Convention on the Elimination of All Discrimination Against Women and Universal Declaration of Human Rights. But poverty and the dangerous environment are real obstacles to women's participation in all aspects of society.

Deniz Kandiyoti has been particularly critical about the slow pace of security and socio-economic conditions; although she believes sustained political and juridical reforms have been achieved.[42] Here, however, I argue that socio-economic progress is the only way to address issues of development, peace and security. Only 3 per cent of women are literate. One woman dies from pregnancy-related causes every thirty minutes. One out of five children dies before the age of five. In many parts of the country where the warlords and Taliban are in charge, women and girls do not go out of the house, fearful for their lives.[43] In this context, talking simply about political and juridical rights is meaningless.

Afghanistan's constitution recognizes the formality of women's rights without having any serious intention of implementing them. Under the US-led invasion, the violation of women's rights continues. Young girls, some as young as seven or eight years old, are sold to secure food for cash. There are no institutions to protect women economically, politically and culturally. Women have been kept in jail for refusing to marry men chosen by their fathers or for refusing to live with abusive husbands. They are accused of endangering the honour of the family and the community. Human rights abuses against women continue to occur with the active support of state institutions such as police, the army and jail keepers.[44]

Feze, an eighteen-year-old woman, was born in Iran, studied and worked in Mashhad. She and her family returned to Afghanistan in 2004. In Iran, her father had allowed her to study and work, but in Kabul, under pressure from the extended family, the father objected to Feze and her sister working. Feze decided to fight against her father and the extended family:

> This is not the father that I knew in Iran. In Iran he did not object to me going to work. Here in Kabul, he says that it is against our family's reputation if I go to work and I should get married with one of my cousins. I objected and continued to work in an internet company. One day when I went back home, I found that my sister had agreed to get married to one of the cousins and my mother has left and gone back to Iran with our little brother. My father said that now that my younger sister had agreed to get married, I had no choice but to follow his orders. But I refused and went back to work. He reported me to the authorities as a 'bad girl' and got me put in jail. In jail I passed the virginity test which is done in jail for all 'bad girls'. But I was kept in jail for months. In jail, I was approached by the jail keeper. When I was finally released from jail, I was approached by the local policeman. When a young woman is accused of being a bad girl by her own father, the word goes around the town that she is available to all men. I am now under constant threat of being murdered by my family as the issue of a woman's honour is linked to the family's honour. I have complained to the Ministry of Women's Affairs. I don't know what will happen to me. They will either kill me or I will win.

The practice of exchanging girls and young women to settle feuds or to repay debts continues, as do the high rates of early and forced marriage.[45] Tahera explained about forced marriages and women's self-burning:

> When someone kills a person, the family of the person who has committed murder force their daughter to marry a man in the other family in the form of compensation. This means the young woman has to marry someone whom she hates and is

> hated by him. In this situation life is so unbearable that many women resort to self-burning. In other cases they escape from their families only to be put in jail when they are found by the police. They spend years in jail and some are raped in jail. When they are released they will be rejected by their families.

In 2005, a woman was sentenced to death in her village. A man in her neighbourhood claimed that in the absence of her husband, she had a sexual relationship with his son. Mahbuba Hoquqmal, the State Minister for Women, blames the prevalence of such incidents on the collapse of the state under the civil war and the Taliban:

> Most marriages and divorces are not registered. This is because throughout the Taliban years the state institutions collapsed. Only people in the neighbourhood were witnesses to any marriage or divorce and sometimes the local clergy was involved. But there was no official registration. It is still the same in many parts of the country. Therefore a man can claim that a woman is or is not married or divorced. If a man claims that a married woman in her husband's absence has had sexual relationship with another man, the woman will be sentenced to death. We face many of these cases in villages and even in some cities.

These cases highlight the importance of socio-economic development and institution-building as preconditions for the real structural change which is currently absent in Afghanistan. The existence of a constitution imposed from above and from outside does not secure women's rights and human rights. According to Hoquqmal:

> Forty years ago we had some of these rights, but that regime was not supported by the people. Now the new constitution has given us rights but we need to make it real through institution-building such as the women's lawyers' society and the women's judges' society. We need to work on women and

> law and children and law. We are working on the UN Convention on the Elimination of All Forms of Discrimination Against Women. We are also working on the issues of violence, marriage, divorce and custody of children. We have women's rights in Islam; the problem is that we have the male interpretation of Islamic law. Nevertheless, we are hopeful that we can change the male interpretation of Islamic laws on these matters.

Since the 1990s, Hoquqmal and other Afghan women have noted a growing interest throughout the Muslim world in Muslim feminists' interpretation of Islamic laws which challenges the conservative male exclusionary and controlling discourse of laws and regulations with regard to women, particularly in Iran where the women's movement has succeeded in reforming laws and regulations in favour of women.[46] Hoquqmal's optimism is, of course, admirable. However, without women's participation in these political processes, no real change will occur to improve women's lives. In fact, her optimism was not shared by many women. For them the promised reconstruction, democracy and women's rights have been limited to a number of elections and seats for women, but not genuine improvement in their living standards. Nasira, a women's rights activist engaged in elections, explained: 'We tried to engage women and men in these elections but they are so poor that they could not pay any attention. They just kept talking about their problems like: food, high rents and bills. When I tried to explain to them about how to obtain electoral cards they said our problem is poverty and lack of food, we don't want any electoral cards.'

Sakina, another woman activist, agreed and similarly argued: 'Even those sections of the community who are not so poor and are educated people and interested in elections are pessimistic and believed that these elections are for the benefit of America because Bush wants to get Afghanistan's election out of his way to show that they have been successful.'

Sima, another activist, optimistically tried to use the elections to raise people's awareness about the future of democracy: 'I tried to convince people that we are responsible for our future. We should be able to rebuild our country ourselves. We should choose our leaders ourselves; we shouldn't let others decide for us. After thirty years, this is a good opportunity for us to think about taking steps towards our future democracy.'

Other women activists used the elections as an opportunity to do political as well as gender consciousness-raising and to encourage women to continue networking. Shafia, an NGO activist, said:

> We have distributed information about different candidates and have tried to encourage women to vote for those whom they think are best candidates for them. Many men think that elections and politics are men's area of concern. So we have discussed with them about women and security and disarmament of different groups. We have used these elections to campaign to free women prisoners who have been kept in jails without any crime. In Kandahar and Kabul we managed to free five of these women.

Shukria Barakzai, who won a seat in the 2005 parliamentary election, is also among the optimists:

> For years we have felt politics with our blood and flesh. We have been fighting and will continue to fight. This is an opportunity for me to raise my voice. We have a good constitution. But women's participation is symbolic. We don't have an independent women's centre. Our streets are full of women beggars and sex workers; we don't have proper health and education. But we are doing our best. Women's and men's views are changing. We can do it.

Despite these women's seeming optimism, there is a growing impatience with a system that has provided many elections but failed to improve living standards.

Again and again, women argue that cultural issues, human rights issues, women's rights issues are cosmetically imposed from above. For them, women's rights include food security, employment, health and education as well as cultural issues. For them, these rights are linked but they prioritized them and emphasized the need for locally appropriate ways of promoting women's rights. Zala in Mazar-e-Sharif argued: 'People are hungry; they talk about women's rights. If real reconstruction takes place we will resolve our cultural problems through the positive side of our Afghan Islamic culture.'

Education

In 2005, 3 million school children and 4 million high school students enrolled and 70,000 teachers returned to work.[47] However, there are shortages of teachers, books, tables, chairs, papers and pencils, let alone other equipment. University courses have closed because of lack of teachers and equipment. The World Bank has confirmed that 'insufficient service provision in rapidly growing cities, inability to afford school expenses and lack of safety and security deter school attendance'.[48]

A number of schools have opened in the cities but these are not enough to meet the demands of the rising population. Many ruined buildings from the war years have been repaired and not rebuilt or reconstructed. Inayattollah from Mazar-e-Sharif explained: 'A few days ago a number of schools' ceilings fell and injured children and teachers because the repair job was not done properly.' In many parts of Afghanistan, even in Kabul, schools use books from the civil war period. Marzia explained: 'These books for primary students read "My parents wake up early in the morning to say their prayers. Russians don't pray, because they are infidel. My father has a gun. He will kill such enemies." These books are worse than useless yet children from an early age are still introduced to "enemy, guns, war and blasphemy" instead of learning anything positive.'

Mansoora, a teacher in Mazar-e-Sharif, said: 'Universities do not have the capacity to absorb the number of candidates and there are no teachers. The salaries of the existing teachers are not paid for months.' Saleha agreed and added: 'Students from Kabul were allowed to sit for entrance examinations but no one from Mazar was able to do so. They didn't print any cards for Mazar students. When we objected they blamed each other. Students went on strike for four or five days, they objected but in the end one year of their life was lost.'

In many parts of the country, parents do not send their daughters to school because it is not safe enough for them to walk there. In the face of invasion, religious and cultural conservatism has increased. Lack of safety, security and service provision are the real reasons for female illiteracy rather than male conservatism. As Sima argued: 'The society can have an enormous influence on all of us as women and men. If there were schools and universities, men won't stop their daughters going to school. Even if they do we could convince them. But there is no security and no facilities.'

Under the Taliban, women taught girls in their homes. Five years after the US-led invasion, there is very little evidence to demonstrate improvements for women's and girls' education. As in the Taliban period, in the majority of cases women have no choice but to teach their children, especially girls, at home. Informal education has now been recognized as the norm in Afghanistan.[49]

Yet, in terms of education at least, change is in the air in Afghanistan. Many women do not think like their mothers and grandmothers. They want to be free and to struggle for their rights. Arian commented: 'Even women in rural areas are willing to send their daughters to school. Those women who have suffered themselves do not let their twelve-year-old daughter get married. They resist the wrong customs. They want their daughters to be healthy and educated. This is a positive change in Afghanistan. We are ready, we need help to stand up on our feet, but no one is helping us.'

Returned refugees

The irony of Afghanistan is that it has massive natural resources. It is a land rich in natural gas, petroleum, coal, copper, chromites, talc, barites, sulphur, lead, zinc, iron ore, salt, precious and semi-precious stones. Afghanistan also has skilled labour, ranging from professionals to industrial and agricultural skills, although the vast majority of these skilled labourers have lived abroad in exile over the last twenty-five years. Five years into the US-led invasion, the Afghan economy is still not functioning and is unable or unwilling to absorb this skilled labour.[50] Refugees have returned with their skills and are willing to participate in the reconstruction of their country, but the doors are shut on them. Ahmed, an educated engineer from America, explained:

> I have offered my services; but they don't want us to participate in the reconstruction. The American government is cooperating with the same commanders and warlords who terrorized women and men during the Taliban. They have mutual interests in sharing the country's resources. They don't want educated Afghan people to go and help the reconstruction of our country. They feel threatened by us. They have shut the doors on us.

Shahla, an educated businesswoman from Britain, said: 'I have come to help with the reconstruction of my country. But there is no place for me here. There is no reconstruction; there is just a terrible rush to make quick money by foreign contractors and a few Afghans. I don't know how long I will survive to remain here.'

Rasoola returned from Peshawar. She was working for one of the local NGOs. She said: 'I am an educated woman. I studied law in Peshawar. My husband is also an educated man but he cannot find a job, we have two children. I am the breadwinner. It is very difficult, as I know that my job in this NGO will not last long.'

Hundreds of thousands of refugees who lived in Pakistan and

Iran have also returned. They are skilled workers but they are not absorbed into the Afghan economy. They, therefore, have no choice but to go back to Iran and Pakistan and work illegally. In Parvan near Kabul, returnees from Iran and Pakistan live in absolute poverty. Sherifa, who returned from Iran, described the situation: 'We had some savings which we brought with us from Iran. We spent all our savings and now we are left with nothing. Many of our friends and extended family have gone back to Iran because our country and our home have been destroyed. There is nothing here for us: no water, no electricity, no homes, no schools, no hospitals.'

Others with more resources insist that they will stay to rebuild their country. Soraya said:

> I lived all my life in Iran, but was never accepted in Iranian society. Now I am living and working in Kabul, here also I am not accepted and do not fit with Afghan society. I am a Farsi/Dari speaker and I love Persian literature. No one can take this away from me, neither the Iranians nor the Afghans. To belong to a common language and a set of common literature is my chosen way of coping with the contradictions of my cultural identity and all the rejections that I have been facing all my life.

Suraya, an eighteen-year-old woman, returned from Iran and worked in one of the HAWCA schools in Kabul. She spoke Farsi with an Iranian accent. In conversation with me she sometimes referred to Afghans as 'them'. I asked her why. She said, 'Because you are Iranian and my accent is the same as yours and not a Dari accent as they speak in Kabul. I, therefore, feel that Afghans are "them" and Iranians are "us".' I asked her whether she would be able to cope with the enormous difficulties around. She said:

> I always heard both positive and negative things about Afghanistan. I always wanted to return. I feel that I belong partly to Afghanistan and partly to Iran. When I was a little girl I always

> felt that I was Iranian. One day at school other children called me 'Afghani'[51] as a derogatory term. I asked why? My teacher explained to me that I am not Iranian. She said I should not be upset when I am called 'Afghani'. From that day I decided that I am not Iranian and I am Afghan and I should be proud of being Afghan. Here they call me Irani in a derogatory way which is also upsetting for me. But I am happy that I have come back to my own country and I am able to help. I am committed to stay to rebuild my country.

However, in the majority of cases, poorer women were better off in Iran and Pakistan, as they worked alongside their husbands and had a better standard of living. In Afghanistan, they had no jobs and had to stay behind with their children while their husbands returned to Iran or Pakistan to work. In the absence of their husbands, they were the head of their households, but felt disempowered as they were unable to work and were the poorest of the poor.

Rogya, also a returnee from Peshawar, said: 'Here in Afghanistan we don't have any land, we don't have a home, so we have to rent a house. But the rent is high. In Pakistan, we worked hard outside and also worked from home. Our children also worked. But we had a reasonable life. Here we have nothing.'

In Kabul and other cities, the returnees live in tents. They face unemployment, lack of education and health. I came across a young man who was begging in the streets. He recognized my Afghan friends who run an NGO in Peshawar. When he was in Peshawar he went to the school provided by this NGO. Back in Kabul, he is a beggar. He felt that he 'was better off in Peshawar as a refugee'.

The population of cities such as Kabul, Mazar-e-Sharif, Jalalabad and other cities is growing fast as the result of the return of the refugees from Pakistan and Iran coupled with massive rural-to-urban migration because of lack of jobs and resources in those areas. Around 1.5 million people come to Kabul from other parts of Afghanistan every year looking for work. Many families move from cold areas to warm areas, as they do not have any way/means of keeping themselves protected from the cold weather in the winter.[52] Those who are extremely poor do not migrate at all and live in absolute poverty.

NATO bombardment in the south of the country as part of the 'war on terror' has led to massive civilian casualties, displacement and migration to Kabul and other cities. All these are migrants faced with unaffordable land and housing. They occupy land illegally and construct houses without official permission. They are, therefore, subject to evacuation. Isolated from their communities and the support system of their extended family, many women become sex workers, beggars or engage in petty crime. Domestic violence is also reported to be high in these communities, although no statistics are available.[53]

The Afghan women and men returnees and those who survived the Taliban period and remained in Afghanistan have the desire to rebuild Afghanistan politically and economically, not in isolation from the global economy but free from the imposed socio-economic and socio-political culture of foreign invaders.

Pornography and Bollywood

The western media, by and large, have reported Afghan's access to satellite television, Bollywood films, mobile phones and the internet as a positive development. Taking into consideration the level of poverty and lack of electricity, very few Afghans actually have access to television stations, mobile phones and internet cafés. For the few who can afford these luxuries, the choice is to watch American-style cop violence movies or Bollywood movies which are an Indian, not a western phenomenon. These movies are particularly popular, as the younger generation can relate to them culturally more than the western films. However, Afghan women's rights activists are concerned about the popularity of Bollywood movies which advocate the subjugation of women to men and the family. Love affairs between a rich man and a poor girl will start with romance, music and dance and will end up in traditional marriage, the wife obeying the husband and his family with the implication of domestic violence if they do not. Homaira, who returned from India, explained: 'There are very good Indian movies. But we only see the films which are about women's subjugation to family. In my view this is even worse than American cop movies, because for ordinary people those films are unrealistic, but they can relate to Indian culture, this can have a more negative impact on people.'

The relative availability of cheap mobile phones for a minority of young men and women in Kabul and a few other urban centres may mean that boys and girls can text each other and meet each other in internet cafés. Many religious conservative families do not consider an internet café an appropriate place for their daughters, as pornography is freely available online in these cafés. Rahima, who went to Mazar-e-Sharif from London to help with the reconstruction of her country, was horrified when one day she went to the local internet café to send emails to her friends and family in London. She described: 'I went to the cabin and pressed the button. I could not believe what I saw on the screen. Obviously the person who used it before me did not turn it off. I was shocked, I kept trying to get out of it and go to emails but it was impossible. I complained to the manager, but he just laughed.'

Mohammad also confirms that people see pornography as an alien western culture and they want to close their doors to it:

> A minority of people watch it at internet cafés curiously as something alien. The same men who watch these don't allow their women to go outside of their front door. In all other societies people have learnt about politics through education and training. In Afghanistan we have learnt politics through wars, conflicts, blood and tears. Afghans are closing their doors and

> bolting them secure from the alien culture which is growing in our society. The changes which are taking place are not according to our culture, we cannot accept them.

Hajara, an NGO activist, confirms that poorer sections of society react to the spread of alien western culture by hanging on to their traditional culture and values more tightly than ever before, sometimes leading to a fanatical conservatism. She describes a horrifying example of the practice of honour killing and female virginity:

> There was a girl who left her home three or four times. The parents sent her to jail. The court decided to do a virginity test on the girl and she passed the test. After that her parents came and took her home. Next we heard that she was poisoned and died. There was no way to prove that the family killed her, no one was arrested and no one was to be blamed. This is the reality of Afghanistan.

Maryam says:

> They have their own agenda and are playing with us like toys in their hands. Under the Mujaheddin and Taliban, they starved us of life. They divided us to rule us. Now they are treating us like starved animals. They have thrown a few mobile phones, internet cafés and Bollywood movies in front of us, keeping us busy in order to steal everything else from us. They have to leave Afghanistan and free us from their domination. Our history has shown that governments which are established by foreigners are not stable governments because Afghans do not accept them. If they read the history of Afghanistan they would understand that Afghans don't let foreigners interfere in their country. One day they will understand that Afghans want freedom from them.

These women's objection to western culture was not dogmatic. They were open to new ideas, but they objected to a neo-conservative agenda to promote a particular culture and understanding of women's rights and democracy which is alien to them. For them, women's rights and democracy had to be contextualized culturally and not dictated from above and from outside. They also gave equal importance to identity issues and material issues. Massouda, who returned from Pakistan, argued that: 'If we use our freedom according to our own culture, we will achieve democracy. On the other hand pornography which is now widespread in Kabul is against our culture and will harm our family and society.'

Shahida, returning from London, has similar views:

> Western culture has both positive and negative sides. We need to adopt the positive side of western culture such as their technology and use it for our development both economically and in terms of health and education. To copy their culture of drink, pornography and nightclubs would be disastrous for our culture. Both of them are called western culture. Unfortunately, our people identify western culture with nightclubs, alcoholic drinks and pornography not the education, technology and other positive aspects of western culture.

Nastaran says:

> Today Kabul is corrupt. People do not have access to food, electricity and water. They hate it when they see the availability of drinks, pornography and nightclubs. There are too many foreigners in Kabul imposing their culture on our young people. We don't feel safe to send our daughters out of the house. We should use their experiences of developments and rebuild our country, not follow them in fashion and the culture of drink, drugs and pornography.

Shahbibi, who returned from London, explained how worried she was about the wrong impression people had about western culture: 'My children are Afghan British. They were educated in the UK, they studied English literature. I want to translate some English literature to Dari to show to young people in Afghanistan that western culture is not about pornography, drink and drugs, it is about Shakespeare, Jane Austen and Charlotte Brontë.'

Is Afghanistan better now?

The more Afghanistan is plunged into poverty and insecurity, the more western media and the politicians emphasize that, despite all problems, it is better now than under the Taliban. The view inside Afghanistan, however, seems to be different. Abdul Satar argued: 'The West created the civil war which then led to the Taliban's rule. During those periods we did not have human relationships. Therefore, obviously it is good that they are not in power. But the new regime has done nothing for us in the last few years. The strategy of the US-led invaders is not to liberate us. It is to strengthen their own position in Afghanistan.'

Arian also argued that:

> The conflict between Pashtun, Hazara, Tajik and Uzbek ethnic groups was mainly because of foreign interventions and the inability of our leaders and religious conservatism. As much as we blame Russian invasion and intervention, we also blame American intervention. They have invaded our country in the name of liberation. They are now turned against some of the same monsters that they created themselves and have allied with some other monsters – the same commanders and warlords, who raped women, murdered their men, stole young women from their families and forced women to leave their husbands and to go with them.

Some women even challenge the terms of the question. Mansoora, working for one of the international NGOs, argued that: 'The Taliban did not allow women out of their houses in order to stop sex work and begging. Today Kabul and other cities are full of sex workers and beggars. Is this better than the period under Taliban? How can I answer this question?' Mohammad, a journalist, agreed: 'People are hungry. Similar to Taliban period they sell their daughters to older men to live on the bride price.' Alama also argued that:

> Very little has changed for us since the fall of Taliban. They keep talking about freeing us from *chaddari*. The reality is that *chaddari* is not our problem; the problem is lack of security, lack of employment, lack of education and health. If we have these then we can sort out the *chaddari* issue, some women may continue to wear it and others may take it off or wear other forms of Islamic cover such as in rural areas.

After the fall of the Taliban, women hoped that they would be compensated for their losses and empowered to participate in the reconstruction of their country. All these factors, however – the opium economy, poverty and unemployment – have not allowed women to put this change in gender relations into effect. In Chapter 2, I argued that under the most adverse conditions of the Taliban regime, Afghan women and men relied upon their social relations and networks of mutual support. They built the foundation for creating social capital which was essential for the process of reconstruction. This was the most important asset through which they kept their families and communities together and enabled them to survive the Taliban regime. With the US-led invasion came poverty, rural-to-urban migration, uprooting, crime, drug addiction, unemployment, alien culture; all these factors are leading to the breakdown of their social relations as their basic safety-net. Growing hostility to the US-led invaders has driven people to sympathize with the Taliban and al-Qaida.[54] It is commonly believed that people work for al-Qaida not because they are terrorists, but because they are desperate: 'If somebody will give me money to put a bomb somewhere, I will do it. That is how it is. My situation is so, that I will do everything that gives me money, and why not join al-Qaida? At least they will provide me some benefit.'[55] Or: 'Only because of our manifold problems, al-Qaida has so many people working for them. But these people are not terrorists;

they are doing it out of despair. If there were only jobs and sufficient income and adequate housing, there would be no more terrorism in Afghanistan.'[56]

Despite the pessimism, these women's voices express an incredible amount of optimism and hope. Women's willingness to participate in the process of reconstruction was very exciting. They hope that their active agency of yesterday and today will take them into the future. Farideh said:

> I was born in Iran and I had never been to Afghanistan. Last year I went to Mazar-e-Sharif where my extended family lives. We went by bus to the Afghanistan border. When we arrived in Afghanistan we all kneeled down to kiss our homeland's earth. As I did this, a wind blew and the earth went into my eyes. I said to myself, I wonder why my homeland throws dust into my eyes. We hired a bus and we went through the mountains and hills. Afghanistan is so beautiful; it is much more beautiful than Iran. We arrived in Mazar-e-Sharif, and my Afghan family did not like the way I was dressed. They said you don't look Afghan, you dress like an Iranian. You speak like an Iranian. I was hurt, but I did not say anything. The day after they brought me a *burqa* and asked me to wear it. I politely refused; I said I have been brought up with the Iranian way of dressing. I am not going to change the way I am. They did not like me saying that, but they did not argue with me. They then said that they are going to the registry office to get me my Afghan Identification Card. I said, I will go with you, they said no, women don't go to the offices to get things done, and men do it for me. Again I objected and said this is my identification card, in Iran I always did my own things myself, so I am going to do this in Afghanistan too. They did not like what I said, but they did not argue with me. So I wore my Iranian dress, went to the office and completed the forms to get my identification card.

Farideh was proud when she was describing this. I asked her whether she could change women's role in society. She replied: 'Yes, I am sure I can, I am not going to change to their way of life. I don't want them to change to my way of life either. I want them to accept me as I am. I know it is difficult, but I am sure patiently I can do it. I have the support of my husband and family.'

Afghanistan today is a country that inspires contradictory feelings. An alien imperialist culture and prefabricated identity wrapped in the rhetoric of 'security, development, women's liberation and democracy' has been imposed on Afghan women and men alike. Afghan women activists' urgent call for economic reconstruction, health and education has fallen on deaf ears. Pornography, violent films, drugs and sex work are widespread.

Yet, since the fall of the Taliban, and in the face of all these problems, Afghan women's activism for structural change has continued. They have found locally appropriate ways of promoting women's rights. Unfortunately, such activism is in constant danger of being eroded by the client state. The Taliban manipulated gender relations in Afghanistan to legitimize their actions. Increasingly, this is a strategy also employed by US policy-makers. Women are denied the right to a voice and to negotiate their identity beyond rhetoric. They are faced with patriarchy, occupation, a lack of social structure and find their culture under attack from an alien regime. They are denied agency in the construction of their new reality. However, they try to continue their agency and autonomy despite the predicament of foreign involvement.

The western doctrine that led to the invasion of Afghanistan was and still is about strengthening US political and economic hegemony and control of the energy resources of the region. Afghan women and men do not have the power to combat them on their own. But they have the power to think and to implement what is best for them and how to construct and develop their country.

They believe that, in their own way and according to their own culture, they could change their communities to accept the participation of women in the economy and society and find legitimate roles for women in the process of reconstruction. The obstacles and challenges they face are not small.

Notes

1 Johnson and Leslie 2004: 11–13; Nawa 2002: 190; Sultan 2002: 202.

2 Afghan Women Mission: www.afghanwomensmission.org; and RAWA: www.rawa.org

3 For details of US bombing of Afghanistan in 2001 see: www.cursor.org/stories/civilian_death.htm; and http://en.wikipediaorg/wiki/war_in_Afghanistan_2001

4 UNDP 2005; and World Bank 2006.

5 CIA Factbook 2005: www.cia.gov/cia/publications/factbook/geos/af.html

6 *Pajhwok Afghan News*, 23 October 2006: www.rawa.org/bamyan_cave.htm

7 In 2005 and 2006, both the Guardian (www.guardian.co.uk/afghanistan) and the Financial Times (www.financialtimes.co.uk/Afghanistan) carried extensive reports on these issues.

8 Rashid 2006.

9 *Financial Times*, 19 February 2007.

10 South Asia Media: www.southasiamedia.net

11 For similar reports, see F. Nawa: www.corpwatch.org; and W. Amani: www.iwpr.net

12 *Guardian*, 20 October 2006.

13 BBC World Service, 8 December 2006; and *USA Today*, 16 November 2006: www.usatoday.com

14 *Guardian*, 30 November 2006.

15 Ibid., 5 December 2006.

16 Johnson and Leslie 2004; see also Jonathan Steel, *Guardian*, 20 October 2006.

17 See Amin 2003; Callinicos 2003; Wood 2003.

18 Stiglitz 2006: 54–6 and 128.

19 Harvey 2005: 82.

20 Harvey 2003: 183–212.

21 Callinicos 2006: 241, 245; and Duffield 2002: 9–17; and Rees 2006: 2, 47, 96–7.

22 Johnson and Leslie 2004: 11; UNSC Resolution 1373, 28 September 2001.

23 During the Taliban rule, the main concern of the international community was for humanitarian intervention in Afghanistan. After 9/11, under pressure from Washington, this position changed to 'security and development'. See Duffield 2002: 15–17.

24 See ibid.: 1–89.

25 World Bank 2004.

26 Aftab 2005: 28–31.

27 Christian Aid 2004.

28 Afghanistan Insurgency Assessment, 2005: www.sensilcouncil.net

29 For criticisms of security in Afghanistan, see Bhatia et al. 2004; and Suhrke 2006.

30 Duffield 2002: 15–17.

31 For a more optimistic but nevertheless critical analysis of the slow process of reconstruction, see Rundle 2004: 179–95.

32 Giustozzi 2004.

33 Human Rights Watch 2004.

34 Asian Development Bank 2005: www.adb.org/Documents/Periodicals/ADB_review/2005/vol37-6/opium-economy.asp

35 For these statistics, see UNODC 2004 and 2006: www.unodc.org; and *Guardian*, 16 September 2006.

36 Aga Khan Development Network 2004: 16.

37 Pain 2004.

38 According to Human Rights Watch 2001, in Kabul alone there are estimated to be some 40,000 widows.

39 UN IRIN 2006; Pain 2004.

40 Viner 2002.

41 Kian-Thiebaut 2005: 95.

42 Kandiyoti 2005.

43 UNDP 2005.

44 Amnesty International 2003.

45 Human Rights Watch Briefing Paper 2004.

46 For the argument about feminist interpretations of Islamic laws, see Abu-Lughod 2002; Ahmed 1999; Hassan 2002; Ebadi 2006; Poya 1999; Rostami-Povey 2001, 2004c or 2004d, 2005; Mir-Hosseini and Tapper 2006; Mir-Hosseini 2002 and 2003.

47 UNDP 2005.

48 World Bank 2004.

49 Kirk and Winthrop 2006.

50 AREU 2005b and 2006a.

51 In Iran and elsewhere, it is common to use the term Afghani for Afghans, similar to the use of Irani for Iranians and Pakistani for Pakistanis. Afghani is the currency of Afghanistan and Afghans therefore find the use of this term offensive.

52 Aftab 2005; and Schutte 2004.

53 World Bank 2004.

54 Barakat 2004: 11–15.

55 Schutte 2004: 24.

56 Ibid.: 25.

4 | Exile and identity

> 'We teach our children and our students that we are Afghans, no matter where we live; we are Afghans.' Bas Gul, a mother and a teacher living in Peshawar

> 'We are *khane be dosh* [nomads] and *sargardan* [wanderers], we feel that our roots are burnt, but we console ourselves with the idea that when we will return we will build Afghanistan as one nation.' Shahbibi Shah, a mother and a writer living in London

The war and conflict in Afghanistan have profoundly shaken the whole of Afghan society and pushed a third of its population into exile. In the early 1980s Afghanistan's population was estimated at 20 million. Since the early 1980s, between 6 and 7 million refugees have settled in Iran and Pakistan and a few hundred thousand in other parts of the region, in the West and in Australia.[1]

This chapter focuses on Afghans who lived in Iran, Pakistan, the UK and the USA. The majority of Afghans in Iran are Shi'a and Hazara, and the majority in Pakistan are Sunni and Pashtun. However, there is a minority of Pashtun in Iran and a minority of Hazara in Pakistan as well as Tajik, Uzbek and Baluch in both countries. The majority in the USA and the UK are middle class and diverse in terms of religion and ethnicity. They also represent two generations of Afghan women.

Migration to Iran and Pakistan

Afghan refugees have left Afghanistan in waves: under the Soviet invasion, during the civil war and during the Taliban era. In 1990, 2,940,000 Afghans lived in Iran and 3,272,000 in Pakistan. Between 1979 and 1992, most Afghans in Iran were given residence and work permits and became eligible for most of the entitlements available to Iranian citizens such as free education and health service, and various state food subsidies. From the mid-1990s, the Iranian government began to withdraw the subsidies to Afghan refugees on the grounds that state expenditure had reached US$10 million per day without any recognition or financial support from the UN High Commissioner for Refugees (UNHCR). Afghan refugees received more education and health services in Iran than in Pakistan. Pakistan has received a large amount of financial assistance from the international community, but Iran did not[2] because the 1979 revolution and the establishment of the Islamic state ended western interests in Iran.

The Pakistani government's policy towards Afghan refugees changed according to the United States' policy. The refugees were welcomed during the civil war when Pakistan supported the Mujaheddin and the Taliban against the Soviet invasion, but between 1988 and 2001 they began placing restrictions on Afghan refugees, and from 2001 onwards they started imposing regulations on them.[3] As a result of these states' policies, by 2000 the number of Afghan refugees had decreased to 1,482,000 in Iran and 2 million in Pakistan. However, there are a large number of Afghans in both these countries who are classified as stateless and not included in the statistics. Despite restrictions on their entry to Iran and Pakistan, harsh conditions in Afghanistan have forced them to move between Afghanistan and these countries as transitory migrant labour. For example, there are an estimated 500,000 people who move backwards and forwards between Iran and Afghanistan[4] and, according to the Afghanistan Research and Evaluation Unit, in Torkham, a border area between Afghanistan and Pakistan, every day 160,000 persons go from Pakistan to Afghanistan and 190,000 persons go from Afghanistan to Pakistan. This is just one border area; the same pattern occurs in other border areas between these countries.[5] The majority of this migrant labour is made up of men; women and children stay behind in Afghanistan as it is easier for men to cross these borders constantly and go to Iran and Pakistan to work. They bring to Afghanistan hundreds of thousands of US dollars per month, and for them and their families this is just survival.

The ethnic composition of Afghans in Iran is 43 per cent Hazara, 31 per cent Tajik, 15 per cent Pashtun, 2 per cent Uzbek and 8 per cent of other ethnic origins, and the majority are Shi'a. In Pakistan it is 82 per cent Pashtun, 7 per cent Tajik and 11 per cent of other ethnic origins and the majority is Sunni.[6] In Iran they are spread over different parts of the county but are mainly concentrated in working-class areas of town and cities such as the capital Tehran, Khorasan near the border with north-west Afghanistan, and Sistan and Baluchistan, near the border with south-west Afghanistan. In Pakistan, they are concentrated in Peshawar, Quetta, Baluchistan near the border with the south-east of Afghanistan and Karachi, which is an important urban trade centre. Although millions of Afghans have lived in Iran and Pakistan since the early 1980s, there is little intermarriage. This is mainly because, despite patriarchal gender relations, many Afghan women see themselves, rather than men, as the bearers of their cultural heritage. In Pakistan, since the fall of the Taliban, intermarriage between Pashtuns from Pakistan and Afghanistan has increased, creating strong ties between the two sides of the border, and against the Afghan central government,[7] an indication of the role of women as bearers of Pashtun culture. There are more marriages between Iranians and Afghans[8] than between Pakistanis and Afghans, especially in Khorasan province where there has been a long history of migration between Iran and Afghanistan since the 1850s.

People from middle-class backgrounds faced a loss of status, being demoted to menial positions in exile, hoping that when they return to Afghanistan they will regain their status. Marzieh described her situation in the 1980s in Kabul in comparison with 2004 in Tehran:

> With a degree in electronic engineering, I taught at Kabul University and then married the man I loved, a university teacher. We had to leave our beautiful home after the USSR invasion. My husband was injured and became disabled. In Iran, I became the head of the family. I hope that when we go back to Afghanistan, my children who are educated in Iran will be able to work in their own profession.

Saleha from Peshawar had similar experiences:

> Eight years ago I came to Peshawar with my family. We had a good life in Afghanistan. My husband and I are educated people; we were working and had a nice home. Here my husband was not able to find an appropriate job and is working as a labourer in the steel industry and I work as a teacher in this school and this way we manage our life. We want to go back but there is nothing for us in Afghanistan.

As the 'Other', in diaspora, women exist on the periphery; they do not find stability in one country. They face racism, prejudice and many social, economic and cultural constraints. Despite historical and cultural ties between the Afghan Shi'a and Iranians and Afghan Sunnis and Pakistanis, Afghans have experienced racism in both of these countries, more in Iran than in Pakistan. As the number of refugees increased in Iran and they were included in the health, education and employment systems, the level of racism against them increased. The media, especially newspapers, were responsible for giving wrong perceptions about Afghans, blaming them for unemployment and crimes. The racism of exile is one of the most painful experiences that Afghan women have faced. Mahtab married an Iranian man and lived in Iran for twenty years. She described how hurtful Iranian racism is for her: 'My accent is neither Afghan nor Iranian. To Iranians I could be either from other cities or other countries. When they ask me where I come from and I say I am Afghan, they turn their backs on me and stop talking to me. Sometimes they start saying nasty things about Afghans, being murderers and so on.'

Only a minority of Afghans in Iran and Pakistan have dual nationality and citizenship rights and only a small number of male workers are integrated into the labour market. The majority of Afghans are forced to live on the margins and the economic hierarchy places them at a disadvantage. They do not have written employment contracts, social protection, social security, insurance or any other benefits and are denied the right to equal wages.[9] Most jobs for Afghan refugees are concentrated in 'ethnic economies': small businesses which depend on the cheap labour provided by a minority ethnic community.[10] In Iran, Afghan men are concentrated in the clothing and shoe manufacturing industries, building, stonemasonry, carpentry and shopkeeping. Women and men also undertake agricultural work and animal husbandry. Those who engaged in farming and agricultural work in Afghanistan have settled in rural areas of Iran and are doing similar work. Afghan women are engaged in teaching, domestic labour, working for NGOs, producing handicrafts, carpet weaving, shelling pistachio nuts and picking zafran.

Zohreh explained: 'My uncles escaped from the Russian invasion, came to Iran and set up a clothes-making workshop where Afghan women and men work. They pay rent to an Iranian owner, but they manage it themselves and provide the labour.' The majority of Afghan women work from home, doing sewing and embroidery, and sell their work in the informal markets. Maliheh said: 'It takes five or six months to sew these classic Baluchi dresses with embroidery. The money that we receive for them is not very much but helps us to support our families.' UNHCR trains Afghan women to teach other languages and computer skills and to produce handicrafts, and helps them to sell their products. Those men and women who do not have citizenship rights work as cheap labour in the building industry. It is not just the economic marginalization, the social and psychological exclusion is equally hard for Afghans. They feel that they contribute to the economy but they are considered to be illegal immigrants. Soraya explained: 'We are cheap labour; we can't claim insurance and other benefits. They say that we don't pay tax either, but we would rather pay tax and be treated equally. We do the work but we are invisible and are perceived as illegal workers. Every now and then the officials attempt to close down Afghan businesses.' Zohal said: 'We feel that we have helped the economy of Iran, we hope that one day the Iranian will realize that their homes, their parks, and their gutters are built and cleaned by Afghans' cheap labour.'[11]

Similarly, in Pakistan, Afghan men are mainly concentrated in low-wage unskilled manual labour in sectors such as construction, market portering, waste collection and recycling. In Karachi, they are concentrated in trade, transport and construction. Poor women are domestic servants and beggars. In Peshawar, the population of Kacha Garhi refugee camp is among the poorest and are engaged in daily wage labour and petty vending. The only community which has access to the blue-collar jobs within the formal sector is the Ismaeli community living in Karachi Metrovile area. Women in this community also have access to jobs in factories, whereas women of other Afghan communities do not.[12] In Haji refugee camp, where the Shi'a community live, the majority of women and male and female children are engaged in carpet weaving. Tahera explained to me: 'These carpets are not ours, we work for factories, we don't have enough wealth to be able to work for ourselves. We work under the factories' contracts. We weave the carpets and our husbands and other male kin sell them to the factories.' I asked her whether she felt it was unfair that women do the work and men receive the money. Her reply highlighted how poverty and hardship can create solidarity between men and women, despite unequal gender relations: 'No. This is our division of labour. What is unfair is economic problems that we are all facing, men, women and children.' Poverty has also forced Afghan communities in Pakistan to be engaged in bonded labour. Nadia, a journalist, commented: 'In a camp near Peshawar, hundreds of Afghan women, men and children work as brick makers. They are indebted to the Pakistani landlord. They constantly borrow money from the landlord for their daily survival. In return, the whole family and community work for the landlord without receiving any wages.'

As in Iran, a significant number of Afghan women are engaged in teaching. Malalai, teaching in one of HAWCA's schools in Peshawar, said: 'These schools are very important for us, because we cannot afford the private education system for our children. Also these schools provide teaching jobs for us, we are refugees, we cannot teach at Pakistani schools. Our salaries are low but it is better than nothing.' During all the years of war and conflict, Afghans, especially Afghan women, were denied education. In diaspora, so many women said: 'The education of our children, especially our daughters, is the most important thing in our life.' In the mid-1990s, when the Iranian government cut subsidies to Afghans' education, Nehzate Savadamozi (the adult literacy movement, a part of the Ministry of Education), and UNICEF joint projects provided some education for Afghans. It was in this period that young Afghan women set up *Madarese Khodgardan* (self-run schools). These young women either were born in Iran or arrived when they were infants and were educated in Iran. Despite racism, many Iranian women helped these Afghan women and a number of film makers have made films about the plight of Afghans in Iran.[13] This made people aware of how unjust is the racist perception of Afghans and increased the number of voluntary workers, especially Iranian women, helping Afghans. In Shahre Ray, near Tehran, a woman and her husband whose job is *lahafdoz* (making traditional duvets) have turned a part of their poor household into a school for Afghan children. Fatemeh said:

> At first the numbers were small but gradually they increased to

> 500. I sought help from Afghan women in the area. This is at a time when the Ministry of Education announced that these schools were not allowed to work because this encourages Afghans to stay in Iran. I went to the Ministry and I argued with them that it is not Islamic to deny them education. I told them that they must give me permission to continue my work. I managed to get some financial help from the Bonyade Zaynab Kobra [Zaynab Kobra Women's NGO] and built a shower in the corner of my house as well so that Afghan children could clean themselves.

In some cases, Iranian private landlords or the local authorities have donated abandoned buildings to be turned into schools for a period of time. In other cases, local mosques have allowed a corner to be used as self-run schools for Afghan children. Fataneh explained:

> I found an old and half-ruined mosque in the area. I got permission from the local authority to use it. I also managed to get a budget to do some repair in the mosque and use it as one of these schools. We managed to teach 130 students in this school. The local authority had to close the school because the roof was not safe. So we moved to another mosque where we used a corner of the mosque as our school. With the help of other Afghan women we have managed to have five classes per day on different shifts. We now accommodate 350 students. We have many more applicants but we cannot accommodate any more and we are trying to set up more schools.

These schools charge according to students' ability to pay. This contribution pays for the cost of running of the schools (rent, electricity, gas, water, repairs and the salaries of the teachers). The teachers' pay in these schools is a fraction of what teachers are paid in Iran, but many Afghan women have volunteered to do this job. Years of war and conflict have determined them to educate themselves and their children, especially their daughters. As a result of their enthusiasm, hundreds of thousands of these schools have been set up across the country. In many cases, these schools operate several different shifts, from seven in the morning until eleven in the evening. Smaller children attend in the morning; older children in the afternoon; women early in the evening; and men late in the evening. Classes are given in literacy and numeracy.

In Pakistan, the education system is mainly private; therefore, only a minority of Afghans have benefited from it. For the majority, education is mainly provided by UNICEF and different Pakistani and Afghan NGOs. There are also the *madrassas*, the religious schools.[14] HAWCA is one of the NGOs operating in Afghanistan and Pakistan. In Peshawar it has two schools, educating 200 children aged between seven and fifteen each year. Salima said: 'In Afghanistan we have two main languages: Pashto and Dari. Here in Peshawar most of the children are Pashto speakers and we teach them Dari. This is a great achievement as we are keeping Dari language alive.' AWN and AWC also provide education and training for young Afghan women and men. In Peshawar, RAWA set up two orphanages. They are funded by their income-generating activities and charity work, including carpet weaving and handicrafts. These two orphanages take care of 100 children who do not have parents or whose parents were disabled during the war or whose parents are so poor that they could not look after them. Arian explained:

> We find these children wandering aimlessly in the streets. We take care of them, teach them and send them to school. They are like our own children. Those who have relatives come to visit and take them out for a day. Others do not have anybody. Most of them have nightmares. They cry and wake up screaming. We try to look after them and give them motherly and fatherly love. In some ways our lives are inseparable from these orphans.

The Afghan women's sense of displacement makes them

want to help these children. With the help of Iranian and Pakistani women's organizations they are able to create community institutions and have provided welfare and charity to care for their community.

Migration to the USA and the UK

In the UK and the USA, the majority of Afghan migrants are middle class and diverse in terms of religion and ethnicity. In contrast to Afghans in Iran and Pakistan, many of whom have no citizenship rights, the majority of Afghans in the West have two passports, making them truly transnational.[15] Most had previously been economically successful and were predominantly educated people from the cities of Kabul, Kandahar, Mazar-e-Sharif, Herat and Jalalabad. In the pre-Soviet era they were the educated middle and upper classes and worked in economic, political, educational and cultural institutions as professionals. Yet Afghans in the UK and the USA have also faced great loss of status. Many live in working-class areas and are engaged in low-paid jobs, especially those with refugee status. As frequently stated by many Afghan women in the UK and the USA, their transition to exile is predominantly affected by their class position back in Afghanistan. This is in contrast to the majority of Afghan women who lived in Iran and Pakistan. This also contests the assumption that immigrants in the West have a more comfortable lifestyle. Suhaila, living in Los Angeles, commented:

> My husband and I are educated and from middle- and upper-class backgrounds. We escaped from the Communist regime in Afghanistan. We worked hard for our survival in America. We were economically and financially demoted. We faced enormous difficulties, working with a small child. I worked during the day and my husband worked in the evening and overnight to be able to survive financially.

This contrast in social status made the racism faced by

Afghan refugees in the West even harder, regardless of their background; the majority of Afghans in the USA and UK are compelled to live in the margins of the exile societies. Many believe that this is because they are forced migrants. Nazia said:

> We are forced migrants; we did not just move from one place to another place, this forced migration affected all aspects of our lives in the new society. We have suffered because the political situation forced us to leave our homes. Also it is not the case that the host country opened their doors to us. We have worked hard in exile; we never worked this hard in Afghanistan. We have brought the richness of our culture and history to these societies as well as money and skills, we work hard, we pay tax and we contribute to the US economy and society.

There have been few intermarriages between Afghans and British and American people. This is mainly a result of cultural division and the West's hostility to people of Islamic culture.[16] Those who did marry Americans or British women and men try to hold on to their Afghan culture, especially the women. But as Nahid described, many mothers were worried about a clash of cultures within these marriages:

> My older daughter has married an American man. He is a nice man and from a good family, but the clash of culture is a real issue. We are very protective of our children; we are scared of some of the negative sides of American culture. All this adjustment is very difficult for our children. My daughter is unhappy because she loves her husband and her parents but the reality is that the two sides are divided.

The majority of Afghan men do not regard Afghan western diaspora women as suitable marriage-partners. In their view, they are too emancipated and too western. Elham, from London, explained:

> I left my parents' house, because they would not let me go out with my British friends. Their plan was to marry me to an Afghan man and if I went out with my friends this meant that no Afghan man would have married me. But I disobeyed them and left home. In their eyes there was no control over me. For me this was hypocrisy as it was OK for the men to go out and by this they were not bringing bad reputation to the family and they would not lose their Afghan identity. But if I or any other young women did the same we would be a disgrace to our families and because we broke the rules we had to lose our Afghan identity.

A significant number of Afghan women in the UK and the USA have married Afghan men from Iran, Pakistan and Afghanistan. Najia, from Los Angeles and head of her family, did not allow her daughter to marry an American, even though he was prepared to become Muslim. She arranged a marriage between her older daughter and a man from Afghanistan whom they had never met, but knew about through the extended family and trusted. She described her feelings:

> I don't trust non-Afghan culture, especially western culture. Many rich Arabs also wanted to marry my daughters but I couldn't do it. Even Arabs are alien to my culture, although they are Muslim. In the West, people don't believe in the continuation of family relationship. They start a relationship easily and they end it easily. In this regard American culture is all about Hi and Bye. I am very happy that my daughter has agreed to an arranged marriage, marrying an Afghan man from Afghanistan.

As I will discuss in more detail later in this chapter, women's resistance to western culture is mainly in response to racism and, in particular, to Islamophobia since 9/11.

As with Afghans in Pakistan and Iran, the education of the young generation, especially girls, is important for parents.

Some Afghans, especially in female-headed households who have settled in the UK and the USA, are relatively poor, but despite financial problems they have made every effort to educate their daughters. Leila explained:

> I worked hard to raise my two daughters, on my own, I was very poor. I received limited help from the state but much help from my extended family and Afghan women's organizations. I used to carry the children on my shoulders and go to buy food for them. I used to have terrible pains from walking long distances and carrying my children everywhere with me in order to do things for them. I worked all my life, I did everything, from washing floors to weaving and knitting and sewing. I made sure that my two daughters got a good education.

Shereno also pointed out that:

> Afghan girls and young women are much more educated than Afghan boys and young men. This is because they see their mothers being weak in comparison with their fathers and do not want to be in the same position. The Afghan young men see their fathers dominating the household and assume that they follow the same path, whether they have education or not.

For Afghan women and men, life in the UK and USA has presented many new roles and demands. Back in Afghanistan, these men were the head of the household. Even in cases where the educated women worked as professionals, men were recognized and respected as the main breadwinners. In exile, many Afghan men have become dependent on women's work and women have become the head of the family. Despite the persistence of traditional gender relations and many women's desire to remain as the bearer of their feminine cultural identity, the change in their socio-economic circumstances has increased their self-confidence and domestic authority. Gender relations between men and women have been altered. The rights of individuals within the household and the family are asserted. Women and men have to renegotiate gendered relationships, as norms and values have changed and they react to these new roles and responsibilities differently. In some cases these changes have created conflicts of interest and objectives within the household, men finding the changes difficult to cope with. Women have responded by finding a new coping strategy based on their traditional feminine response. Halima explained: 'I want recognition as his equal not as his superior. It is not his fault that he has lost his status. In Afghanistan he had more opportunity, here he had less. I don't want to reverse our roles. I want harmony in my family.' Afghan women insist on harmony rather than more conflicts in their households. They find the western concept of individualism to be at odds with their Afghan communal identity; in some ways this is more important for women than men.

Zainab looks after her family in London. To a certain extent, she supports an individual's right to make choices within the family, but not at the expense of losing control over the social aspects of family life:

> I have tried to learn the positive sides of British culture and hang on to the positive side of my Afghan culture. I have come to the conclusion that a level of individuality is good. I sometimes feel that my British individual identity is in opposition to my Afghan communal identity. For example, I am thirty years of age but I live with my parents. I am not married. I have chosen not to get married and instead to look after my parents. I work and contribute to the family's budget. I have my own room. They don't interfere with what I do. But they want me to get married and have my own family. For them religion is part of the family's day-to-day affairs. For me religion is deep in me. But I am not a religious person. I pray when I can. All these differences between us are sometimes in conflict with each other. But this is the best I can do, a mix of individuality and communal life. This way I feel that I am picking the best of both worlds.

Years of exile have had a strong impact on Afghan women's identities, changing their way of life. They have adopted social and economic roles which are vastly different from those experienced in Afghanistan. The material conditions of migration have created a different understanding of identity, family and community relationships, individualism, self-fulfilment and how future Afghan society should be organized and what meaning the institutions which support society should carry. However, their reaction to individualism, especially in the West, is to give it a cautious welcome at best. They do not want the expansion of individual choice to lead to the loss of their communal interests. Years of exile have not taken away from them the essence of the way they see the world – always being and sharing with others.

Diasporic consciousness in Iran and Pakistan

The relationship between the trauma of displacement and the identity processes involved in rebuilding a life is well documented.[17] For many Afghans, their most painful memory is of the loss of homeland. Hajara feels that the loss of homeland is worse than the loss of her father and brother, 'because they were martyred for our homeland, but when we were forced to leave our country, we lost everything. At first even thinking about living in Pakistan was painful. But when we came here we tried to adapt ourselves to our new situation. Gradually we found that we can have a life here.'

Despite many economic and social constraints and racial exclusion, the first generation prefers exile to years of war and violent conflict in Afghanistan. Their perception of what constitutes exile and where is home depends on diverse factors such as age, class, ethnicity and religion, as well as the racism they suffer in exile and the conflict they experienced at home. Afghan Hazaras in Mashhad in Iran and Pashtuns in Peshawar in Pakistan are particularly keen to remain where they are, partly because of their historic ethnic and religious ties and partly because they have been persecuted in Afghanistan. Fatana expressed her feelings: 'I cannot forgive and forget what they did to the Hazaras. I can live with Iranian racism but I cannot live with any more war, ethnic violence and foreign invasion.' Similarly, Zaynab, a Pashtun woman living in Peshawar, said: 'Despite racism, Pakistan is my home, it has provided the things that we expected from our own country, I don't have any good memories from Afghanistan, all I remember is the way my father was killed and my mother and my sister and brother were injured and how our house was ruined.' Afghan refugees who came originally from poorer or rural areas of Afghanistan and have experienced a better standard of living in exile, also do not want to go back, especially the children of refugees who have heard that there is no shelter, employment or security in Afghanistan. Adela from Peshawar said: 'I like Pakistan. I have had a good life in Pakistan. At the moment I don't want to go to Afghanistan, I want to go back when I can have a comfortable life in Afghanistan.'[18] However, for the younger generation who arrived early in infancy or who were born in exile, integration is painful. Farideh explained her childhood experiences:

> At school and at university and in the dormitory of the university I felt that I was Iranian. But at home I felt that I was Afghan. It is a good feeling to belong to two cultures. However, I felt racism and prejudice from my friends and classmates. I decided not to tell them that I am Afghan. It was easier to hide my Afghan identity as I witnessed how Afghan children and young people were bullied and were insulted.

Although Hanifa enjoys her life in Pakistan, she feels that Afghanistan is her home:

> Home for us is Afghanistan even if there is nowhere for us to live and no jobs to go to. But it is always my home. I always carry with me my Afghan culture; by that I mean my Afghan way of life, which is very different from Pakistan's way of life.

> Here they look down at us for our way of life. They feel they are superior to us and we are inferior to them. In these seven years that we have lived in Pakistan, to adapt to the Pakistani culture and hang on to our own way of life has been very difficult.

Sima, from a middle-class background in Afghanistan, who went to university in Iran, feels hurt that she has been rejected by Iranian society: 'Iran has provided opportunities for us to study but we are still outsiders here. We are not accepted in this society and we have no future here. This is painful and disappointing. I am a qualified nurse and my husband has a degree in agriculture, but we have no future in Iran.'

Young Afghans feel rejected in the exile societies and find themselves constantly negotiating between their home country and their adopted country. Sherifa said:

> I prefer to live in Karachi. But I always feel that one day I have to go back to Afghanistan. When I went back to Afghanistan, I did not feel at home either. Many were hostile to us and believed that we escaped to have a good life in Pakistan. They don't understand that nowhere is like home, but we have one foot here and one foot there, which is very painful.

For children, integration is even more difficult; they find themselves caught in the middle of a battle, trying to hold on to their Afghan identity while accepting their Iranian or Pakistani identity. In Iran they speak Farsi with local Iranian accents. In Pakistan they speak Urdu and Pashto and not Dari. Most do not have a grasp of Afghanistan as their native country,[19] yet they still insisted on saying, 'I am Afghan.'

The majority of the younger generation have never felt fully integrated and have remained isolated, caught between two very different societies (Afghanistan and Iran; Afghanistan and Pakistan). Suraya, who was born in Iran, described her feeling of isolation and confusion: 'Sometimes I wish I was not Afghan, sometimes I feel I don't want to be Iranian. Sometimes I wish those borders between Iran and Afghanistan did not exist. Those borders are very painful.'

These stories demonstrate Afghans' nomadic existence in the margins of exile societies. Some stories are about survival but others are about acquiring knowledge and empowerment. Despite racism and marginalization, Afghan women have shown great resilience and have challenged their portrayal as vulnerable and passive victims. In this way they have become advocates of social change. As individuals, as well as in networks and organizations, they have reinvented the institutions of social life in order to survive. They have sought to turn the void of exile into positive negotiating space for creating new identities.[20]

When I visited one of the joint UNICEF/Iranian Adult Literacy Organization schools funded by the UK Department for International Development (DFID) in Iran, Fataneh, a young Afghan female student, criticized the powerful international institutions and questioned their role in helping children like her. She said to the UNICEF worker: 'What is the point of making wars and creating needy children and then creating budgets to help the needy children?' Exile has created a sense of solidarity with other exile and refugee communities as well as a strong feeling of Afghanness. Zohreh made the connection between Afghans and Palestinian refugees and expressed sympathy with Iraqis and Palestinians. She admitted that, back in Afghanistan, hostility towards Arabs and Palestinians was unjustified:

> In Afghanistan many of us felt that the Arabs (some Taliban) were the occupying forces in our country and we felt that over the years Palestinians have been given more attention by the media and the international community than the Afghans. But now we feel solidarity with the Palestinians and the Iraqis whose lands and countries have been occupied by hostile forces and violence has been used against them.

These Afghan women's experiences, therefore, seem to corroborate Edward Said's powerful claim:

> Exile forces us to see things not simply as they are, but as they have come to be that way. Situations that mould cultures and societies are not inevitable but are a series of historical choices made by men and women, facts of society made by human beings not as natural or God-given, therefore unchangeable, permanent, irreversible. Exile means that you are always going to be marginal, but that you will also embark on nomadic roads that will lead to more knowledge and empowerment.[21]

Exile, history and Afghan futures

To overcome their alienation and marginalization, Afghan women, especially the younger generation, have sought a new identity which can provide them with new agency. In Afghanistan they were divided according to specific forms of identity: ethnic (Pashtun, Tajik, Hazara, Uzbek); religious (Sunni, Shi'a); class; generation; language (Pashto, Dari, Uzbeki). In exile, however, they are all identified as Afghans, they have to speak the languages of exile (Farsi, Urdu and English) and are subject to Iranian, Pakistani, British and American racism. They have reformulated their identity into a multiple identity made up of their past history and present circumstances, and have tried to rebuild life and renegotiate gender roles according to their own culture.[22] For many, the negative aspects of the violent conflicts of the past and the racism of exile societies are experiences to be put to use to build a better Afghanistan – Afghanistan as a nation. These women are neither romanticizing nor neglecting the past but trying to mix the best of each to create a cultural space of active agency in which they can shape a better future.

This was described by Tahera: 'Here as Tajik, Pashtun and other ethnic groups we live together and work together, as one community, the exile/refugee/diaspora community. Together we feel a different form of racism – Pakistani racism against Afghans. So we have learned that racism and ethnic conflicts are devastating and we can live together as a nation without conflict.' Zubair had a similar experience: 'Here in Karachi my

Uzbek and Tajik friends accept me as their brother and welcome me in their household. When I went back to Kabul, I experienced the same among those who have returned from exile.'

Indeed, when I visited Al-Asif Square Afghan settlement in Karachi I could see that five different ethnicities lived in the same building or next to each other in harmony. Fatana said: 'We live together and we work together. We are aware of each other's problems and we try to resolve our problems, despite ethnic, language and religious divides. What is important for us is that we are all Afghans and Muslim.' The younger generation, who have lived most of their lives in Iran or were born in Iran, also did not feel hostile towards each other in terms of ethnicity or religion. They feel they are Afghans in exile. For them, the Muslim collective identity is a reaction to the racism of exile society and the history of violent conflict in Afghanistan. For them, Muslim collective identity is empowering, enabling them to move away from divisive ethnic identity and to find their Afghanness. Zahra argued: 'When we hear from our parents about warlordism and ethnic tension we can see the negative impact of this position and we have learned that it is possible to live together without hostility, violence and tension. We feel that we can take this with us to Afghanistan and try to end warlordism and violence between different groups.' Mansoora, however, has a more cautious optimism and points out that, among the exiles, ethnic and religious associations and prejudices still exist:

> Unfortunately we have a history of ethnic conflicts. Pashtuns against Hazara, Hazara against Pashtun, Tajik against Pashtun and Pashtun against Tajik and so on. In exile, there is no violent conflict among us, but we only socialize with and support our own community. For example, if you want to look for a job, if you are Dari, you approach Dari people and if you are Pashtun, you try to approach Pashtun people, because you have a better chance of getting help from your own community.

Nevertheless, Rasoola believed that ethnic conflicts among

Pashtun, Uzbek, Tajik and Hazara are the result of foreign intervention. Fatana, though, challenged the idea that Afghans' problems can all be associated with external forces. She emphasized that 'if there was not such a degree of ethnic conflict in Afghanistan, we would not be in this present situation', but her friend Sakina, who is working with an Afghan NGO, stressed that:

> Despite the persistence of religious and ethnic associations and divides, exile has forced them to think about Afghanistan as a nation. In this organization and with networking with other Afghan and Pakistani NGOs we work with different ethnic groups. Here we all feel Pakistani prejudices and racism; this has created a degree of solidarity between us and making us think of ourselves as a nation, despite all the different prejudices among ourselves.

For many, the feeling of being Afghan first and then Pashtun, Hazara, Tajik or Uzbek, gives them freedom; it is a window of opportunity for them to find a meeting point of different cultures. For them, the negative aspects of the violent conflicts of the past and the racism of exile societies are experiences that bridge the present and the past in order to shape the future.[23] Maliheh (a Tajik and Sunni) married her husband (a Hazara and Shi'a) in the 1970s in Kabul and went to Iran after the Russian invasion. She said:

> We fell in love and we married against the will of our families. We respect each other's religion and we have left our children to choose whether they want to be Shi'a or Sunni. One of them prays in Shi'a way, the other prays in Sunni way and two of them do not pray at all. In Afghanistan we faced violent conflicts. Here in Iran there is no violent conflict but there is prejudice and racism. As a Sunni I feel insulted because of the tradition of *Omar Koshy*, where in some parts of the country and among the traditional communities they burn Omar [a

> Sunni leader of early Islam] rag dolls during the month of *Moharam* [Shi'a remembrance of the killing of their leaders in early Islam].[24] The experiences of violent conflicts in the past and racism of the present have taught me a lesson that I can take with me to Afghanistan and use to fight against ethnic and religious violence and racism.

The younger generation, in particular, feel able to rise above ethnic and religious tensions. Najibeh explained her relationship with her best friend:

> I am Sunni and my best friend is Shi'a. We have two different cultures and religious values. But we give each other the right to follow our own culture and values which are different and we have decided not to talk about those issues which may divide us. Instead we share those cultural values that we both follow. As a result we are the best of friends and hope to take this experience to Afghanistan.

The younger generation's hope for Afghanistan as a nation is built upon the image of Afghanistan drawn for them by the first generation. For the older generation the coping strategy is to perceive themselves as cultural guardians. This strategy has enabled them to maintain memories of the homeland in order to hold their families and communities together. Women's notion of remembering Afghanistan and teaching their children about Afghanistan involves resisting the uprootedness and racism of exile societies. In turn, this strategy has empowered many to conceptualize new ways of studying their past as well as planning for their future. By working in *Madarese Khodgardan* in Iran and by engaging with Iranian, Afghan and Pakistani women's NGOs and women's organizations, they have learned leadership skills and community work. The provision of education by NGOs in Pakistan and by *Madarese Khodgardan* has been limited but they have provided opportunities for them to overcome the limitation of education systems in exile which have created cultural boundaries and made their children outsiders. They have taught their children about Afghanistan as a nation with diverse peoples. Sima said:

> These schools have very few resources, small rooms, not enough light, no playground, torn books donated from Iranian schools, hot in the summer, cold in the winter. However, the good thing about these schools is that different Afghan ethnic groups have come together to study and to teach about our homeland. Our parents may have prejudices against each other but children do not. We can take this experience to Afghanistan and show that we can live together in harmony.

These new identities as Afghans and Muslims are the product of such experiences of exile. By listening to women's stories, I learned about their deep-rooted understanding of their history and their desire to teach their children about their history as a site of struggle and resistance. Bas Gul, a mother and a teacher in Peshawar, said: 'We teach our children and our students that we are Afghans; no matter where we live, we are Afghans.' Habibeh, teaching in Tehran, speaks Farsi with an Iranian accent, the same as her students; but her parents and the grandparents of her students speak Dari. She explained how she tries to speak with a Dari accent, not to romanticize her Afghan heritage but to synthesize the past and the present to build a bridge between different generations for the future of Afghanistan: 'When I teach I try to change my accent from Farsi to Dari, but it is not easy. I am Tajik and Sunni, but when children ask me what I am I say I am Muslim and Afghan like all of you.'

Changing gender relations in the context of Islamic culture

Afghan women have been weaving together the threads of the past and present, Pakistani/Iranian and Afghan cultures, and have been negotiating to create a milieu in which they can overcome their alienation. In this process, their survival strategies have broadened to incorporate the struggle for gender rights and they have questioned male authority, fighting to break free from confining traditions, male domination and a life of marginalization. This is especially true in Iran because of the experience of the women's movement there[25] and the support-that they have had from women's NGOs in Iran and Pakistan that have assisted and encouraged them in their task.

Afghan women in Iran and Pakistan define gender relations sometimes in the context of greater gender equality and sometimes in terms of their own complex understanding of how gender relates to Afghan identity. This has enabled them to negotiate the relationship between patriarchy and Islam. They do not regard conforming to traditional Pakistani and Iranian Islamic dress codes, including the head scarf, as cultural constraints, oppression or patriarchy (concepts used in the West). They define their goal and social relations as an attempt to create a more progressive Afghan society where women have access to healthcare, education and employment. Marzia emphasized:

> In exile we have realized the importance of education for women. In Afghanistan we accepted when they told us that education is against religion, against Islam, especially for women. Now we have realized that education is not against Islam, education will make us realize that ethnic and religious conflicts could be eradicated, especially if different ethnic and religious groups are given equality of opportunity in economic participation. This way we could also move towards nation building, and to move away from ethnic and religious conflicts.

Sakina explained how the ideology of the women's movement has had a significant impact on diaspora gender relations:

> I went to Iranian school for three years, but my father did not let me continue my education. He said I am becoming too tall. I was very upset. I was wondering why my Iranian friends go to

> school and they are all the same height as me. I was envious of them. But I could not object to my father's decision. I am now continuing my education at adult literacy classes, alongside my parents. Sometimes my father says women have to stay at home. I say to him no, women in Iran go to school and to work, because nowhere in the Qur'an and Islam does it say that girls cannot go to school or should not go to work. He doesn't argue with me any more. When we go back to Afghanistan, I will be a teacher and will certainly try to change men's views about girls' education and women's employment.

Women in Iran have a relatively equal status with men within the family, education and employment. This has motivated many Afghan women to fight for their rights. Fahimeh believed that:

> Many young people who have lived in Iran for long years see the women's movement and how women are much better off here than in Afghanistan. They are not going to allow Afghan men to behave the way they behaved towards their mothers. We have witnessed that in Iran; women have been fighting for their rights and have been successful. This is an important experience to take with us to Afghanistan.

Maryam also argued that:

> In many parts of Afghanistan families and men do not want their women to go to school, to go to work and even to be seen by a male doctor. Under these circumstances, it is difficult for women to break these deeply rooted traditions. But the experience of living in an Islamic country where women go to school and to work is important; our experience can have an impact on Afghan society. We can change the anti-women traditions. We cannot be aggressive about it, we need to work on it hard and convince those women and men about the benefits of women's participation in society.

Afghan women are not passive victims of male domination,

religion and tradition; many Afghan men are not aggressive and oppressive, as in popular western perceptions. Gender relations are not fixed, given and unchangeable. Shaima explained how her mother – a Pashtun woman – as the head of the family resisted gender and ethnicity pressures:

> Some of our neighbours in Peshawar were talking behind our back, saying their mother works to bring up her children on her own. She should get married. Some of our extended family pressurized her to get married with a rich man to bring us up; she refused. They pressurized me and my sister to marry Afghan men living in the West. My mother refused. They pressurized my brother to leave his study and open a shop. My mother resisted. Thanks to her we are all educated and independent. My mother is not the only one, there are many Pashtun women like my mother. My cousin is also the head of her family, and she is a doctor. This is despite the fact that some of our relatives are very conservative, especially the men; they believe women should not go out of the house.

In Iran, the age of marriage among the Afghan community is lower than the national age of consent, which is twenty-two.[26] However, I met Hazara and Pashtun women who are in their late twenties and are not married or are married but decided to have children later in their married life. I asked whether they had been pressurized by the family and the community. Halimeh, a Pashtun woman from Khorasan who is not married, replied: 'No, they don't pressurize me. I have had many proposals but I have refused them and my family have left it to me to decide when and to whom to get married.' In Iran, urbanization, economic and human development (health, education and employment) have led to the rise of nuclear families and a decline in extended family relationships. Many in the younger generation have welcomed their individual rights. Other Afghan young women, however, feel that they adopt these individual rights only according to their own culture. Salime explained:

> There are many positive sides to the Iranian culture which I try to follow. I also follow the positive sides of my Afghan culture and make them complementary to each other. For example, family relationships among the Afghan communities in Iran are stronger than among the Iranians. I prefer the Afghan way of close family relationships. It is customary among the Afghan young people to consult with the older people in the family and community when they want to get married. Young people in Iran do not practise this custom as much as we do and the rate of divorce is higher among the Iranians than the Afghans. I prefer the Afghan way. I agree that the older people should not intervene in the life of younger people. But young people should consult with the older people for their own good.

Similarly, Farida felt that women are better off in Pakistan's traditional setting: 'In Pakistan, women are respected and have a special place in society. In public places such as banks or shops where men and women queue, women always go first; this is positive as women feel respected among strange men. Here in Pakistan women are respected more than in Iran. I was shocked when I was in Iran to see that the custom of "ladies first" does not exist.'

Women see some aspects of traditional gender relations, such as sex segregation, including covering the woman's body, as empowering. Najia explained how when she travels between Pakistan and Afghanistan the security officers do not touch women and treat them with respect, while they give men a hard time: 'When we want to pass the borders, women easily go through but police stop men, check them and force men to bribe them. They don't do this to women.' I asked her whether this might be because men believe women are the weak sex and need protection. She replied: 'No. It is more positive than negative. These men respect women. It is true that they think that women should go home quicker and do their housework. But generally it is more positive. Anyway, it is good to get home quickly and get on with your other work. Otherwise you have to work longer hours.'

Afghan women's mobilization for survival around *Madarese Khodgardan* in Iran and Afghan women's engagement with Iranian, Afghan and Pakistani NGOs and women's organizations extended to their struggle for women's rights. These organizations, as Salima from Sherkatgah NGO explained, 'produced publications for women and provide advice about marriage, divorce, custody of children and other family issues in Pakistan'. Hami NGO in Iran financially supported some of the *Madarese Khodgardan*. Nahid, the director of Hami NGO, explained how networking with Afghan women was beneficial for Iranian women:

> After the fall of the Taliban, we organized a few conferences in Tehran and Mashhad to engage Afghan women in Iran in the Loya Jirga. We invited Afghan women lawyers to Iran to discuss women's health, education and employment with the refugee communities in Iran. We also benefited from this relationship because we also showed to our own system that it is important to have women judges and to recognize the importance of having female judges in the Iranian constitution.

The Iranian NGO Training Centre (INGOTC) organizes training sessions for women's NGOs and supports Afghan women's activities. Afghan Women Network (AWN) manages networking between different Afghan and Pakistani NGOs inside and outside of Afghanistan. The support of these women's organizations has encouraged Afghan women to extend their struggle for gender equality in the private sphere into the public sphere. These women have tried to change the patriarchal gender relations that recognize only men as breadwinners, heads of households and decision makers. They have formed new and diverse conceptions about identity and agency, but they negotiate gender roles according to their own culture. Massuda is the head of an orphanage in Peshawar and her husband is her assistant. When she goes out of the house, her husband accompanies her according to the Afghan concept of *mahram*. I asked her whether this practice limits her mobility because it considers men to be protectors of women. In response she defended their way of gender power relations:

> My husband agrees with our work arrangement, I am in charge and he helps me. People think that Afghan men are bad men, this is not the case. During the Taliban's period they supported women's activities. They also help us with the housework although it's not in their culture. Afghan women in Pakistan are not free to go wherever they want to without *mahram*. This is our culture. When we want to go somewhere they come with us so in this way they cooperate with us.

These women know the importance of breaking down traditional barriers in order to change their world. For them it is hard, but not impossible, to modify gender relations. Men's perception of women's place in the home and men's place outside it can be changed only by convincing them that women's participation in the economy and society is important for women, men and children, in fact the whole community. In Halima's view:

> Human beings are flexible and if we do things in the right way, we will succeed. We have to go back to Afghanistan, to live there and work hard for our society. We can show to men not just by words but through our activities and our experiences that women's education, health and employment is good for the whole society. When they see the result, they will accept.

Economic necessity in exile changed women's and men's position within the community. Zarghuna described her own situation: 'I am the head of my family, I am the breadwinner and there are many of us. The society has to accept it. There is no choice.' Leila agreed: 'In most cases men and women work because economic life in exile is difficult. Everything is expensive. Children going to school need bags, notebooks, pencils and pens. We also have to pay for water, electricity and gas. Men's wages alone are not enough. It will be the same in Afghanistan. There is no choice.' Some men accept women's work out of economic necessity rather than adherence to the notion of 'women's rights'. However, as Fahima stated, many Afghan women believe that cultural change brought about by economic necessity will be sustained beyond such immediate need:

> Today in Pakistan and Afghanistan, women are working outside [the home]. This is not because men have accepted this as a woman's right. They are forced to accept it because of economic problems in spite of their culture. But I think if women use their freedom in a positive way in the future, men will accept with their heart. For example, when we were in Kabul, I was going to work, one of my neighbours was critical of me and laughed at me but now I know that his wife is working in Pakistan; he hasn't changed his views yet, this is only because of economic pressure in their life and they don't have any other choice.

Talking with a number of men revealed how women's resistance to male domination within the Islamic context, together with economic pressures, have affected traditional gender relations and the idea of masculine protection of women and family. Afghan men in Iran and Pakistan are relatively open to new ideas and are willing to recognize women's rights and value their contribution to the family and society. Ahmed – a fifty-year-old Pashtun man and father of five children – argued that 'today women work hard for the family. They tolerate many difficulties. Of course, we respect them and value their work.' Zala said: 'My husband respects women workers. He says, women are one wing of the bird and men are the other wing. A bird cannot fly only with one wing and a society cannot progress without women.' Women's agency is also influenced by their increasing involvement in collective activities. Many feel empowered when, as women, they struggle together against their common oppression. Sakkineh is engaged in drugs and HIV/AIDS awareness campaigns in Iran. She explained that 'when we visit families to distribute free condoms, women and men feel shy but they do listen and welcome us'. I asked how successful she is in her campaign to convince women to refuse to have sex with men if they don't use condoms. She replied: 'It is difficult for women, some do and some don't, but we continue to visit them and discuss with them and we will make sure that they feel confident about standing up for their rights.'

Women activists have used elections in Afghanistan as an opportunity to engage diaspora women with political campaigning, consciousness-raising activities and networking with women in Afghanistan. For other women, these elections provided an opportunity to convince male kin that women's work is important. Zahra explained:

> My brother, who is the head of our household since the death of my father, would not let me to go to work. He believes that women should only work in state-run enterprises[27] and it is hard for Afghans to find jobs in state institutions in Iran. During the elections, myself and other Afghan women argued with my brother and convinced him that this is similar to governmental work and he agreed. I intend to argue with him and convince him that I should continue to work in enterprises other than the state enterprises.

In Iran and Pakistan, Afghan women's different spheres of life (the domestic sphere, the ethnic community, the concepts of homeland and diaspora) all are social sites of gendered struggle where Afghan women challenge male, ethnic, age and religious domination. They have more opportunities to struggle for their gender rights within the domestic sphere and the ethnic community.[28] As will be discussed in the next section, in the UK and the USA, this task is much harder for them. Many, perhaps most, of the life narratives of Afghans in the UK and the USA represent the tensions between notions of 'tradition' and 'modernity' in the context of their identities, especially gender identities.

Diasporic consciousness: the impact of 9/11 and 7/7 on Afghan women

Like Afghans living in Iran and Pakistan, many Afghans in the UK and the USA have experienced the trauma of displacement and identity confusion. They find belonging to the diaspora community the most important coping strategy. Nastaran, an upper-class, middle-aged woman settled in Queensway, a middle-class neighbourhood in London, in the late 1980s. She felt depressed: 'I had to move out of this affluent part of London and to move to the working-class part of West London where most Afghans and Asian communities live. I could not cope with my nice house; I had to be with my community.' To find a space where they can merge the oppositional worlds of home and exile is even harder for the younger generation. Saleha explained:

> I was fourteen when I left Kabul, when I was packing I left my personal things, hoping that our departure would be temporary. Life in London was a culture shock. I tried very hard to cope with the shock for a long time. The separation from my friends and extended family was very hard. Here at school, children were rude to their teachers and to each other. I could not understand this. We were polite to our teachers and we were close with our friends at school. In Afghanistan, life was social and communal, we did not feel individuality. London was the opposite. It was a real struggle to rebuild my life.

Nasira's experience of her school days was similar:

> I always wore trousers, my school mates kept asking me why I wore trousers and not short skirts. This was a big deal for them but not for me, I could not understand why they are so obsessed with what we wear. Our English was not good but we

> were good at mathematics, science and sports. In fact, what we learned at high school in Afghanistan they teach at university level here. So we tried to learn English but also relied on our strength. They tried to bully us but we stood against them. They could not understand that we had seen wars and conflicts; we were not scared of their bullying behaviour. So after a while they left us alone. But all of that was very difficult.

Shahbibi Shah moved to London with her family in the early 1980s. She experienced a horrific form of racism when her husband's nephew was murdered in a racist attack. She writes:

> Ruhullah was trapped by a gang of fourteen racists armed with makeshift clubs and iron bars just outside his family's flat. He was twenty-four years old, very talented, planning to be a doctor, gentle, peace-loving and very handsome. His life support machine was switched off after four days and he died ... That day we were left with a lifetime of grieving. A light went out – a good life was wasted for nothing. Perhaps it was his destiny that dragged him all the way from our war-torn country to lie in a pool of blood and die on the streets of a civilized one.[29]

These horrifying incidents in the 1980s and 1990s were relatively isolated cases. The attacks in New York on 11 September 2001 (9/11) and 7 July 2005 in London (7/7) have led to racist attacks against people of Islamic culture in the USA and UK on a large scale.[30] Following these events, a new Islamophobia, with its roots in the colonial period,[31] provided an identity ('them') to build the identity 'us'. Islam is portrayed as an antagonistic political force, not compatible with western modernity ('our way of life'). Muslims are represented as a different and inferior Other, unable to embrace women's liberation and democracy. A space has opened up for 'waging the battle of the twenty-first century against the enemy of civilization – Islamic terrorism'.[32] Afghans, and Afghan women in particular, have been at the receiving end of these ideological offensives as a result of their perceived association with the Taliban, al-Qaida and terrorism and have been physically and emotionally abused, especially those Afghan women who wear the *hijab*.

For Muslim women, the *hijab* represents the Islamic concept of modesty. Despite this commonality, the practice of wearing the *hijab* is diverse throughout the Muslim world, depending on local styles of clothing and local interpretations. The majority of practising Muslim women wear the *hijab* as a matter of personal choice and as an expression of one of many of their identities. Through *hijab*, they communicate their pride in their Muslim identity. For them it has positive meanings, regardless of whether or not or how they wear it. Those who choose to wear it find it emancipatory and for some it symbolizes their resistance to western imperial hegemony and the hysteria of Islamophobia. These women challenge the western concept of freeing the female body from the *hijab*. For them, the female body desires freedom from war, rape and unwanted pregnancy and not *hijab*.[33]

In the West, the *hijab* of Muslim women is simplistically interpreted as an imposition by patriarchal Muslim men, enforcing the submission of Muslim women; all Muslim women are seen as being oppressed by tyrannical Muslim men, and the *hijab* seems to epitomize Islamic cultural inferiority. This Orientalist view portrays the Muslim women as having no voice. In post-9/11 and -7/7, the *hijab* is used as a tool to portray Muslim women, in particular Afghan practising Muslim women, as the barbarian Other, who should be kept in check. The impact of the media on creating negative perceptions in the West has certainly contributed to the new Islamophobia and a decline in rational thinking.

The redefinition of Afghan communities post-9/11 is painful for women. Alama from Los Angeles, whose mother wears the *hijab*, said: 'They look at us as terrorists and they blame us for 9/11. My mother wears a scarf and when she comes to school many are abusive to her. They are really racist and ignorant.' Fariba similarly argued that: 'The term "Muslim terrorist" suddenly became popular. They never use the term "Christian terrorist" or "Jewish terrorist". This is a new and particular form of racism.'

These new sentiments are incomparably worse than the prejudice and racism that Afghan women faced in the UK and the USA prior to 9/11 and 7/7; nor are they comparable to the prejudice and racism that Afghans faced in Iran and Pakistan. Despite Iranian and Pakistani racism and chauvinism, in the face of growing Islamophobia people in Muslim majority societies have embraced a collective Islamic culture. Afghans in the West now feel solidarity with Palestinians and Iraqis, as do the Afghans in Iran and Pakistan quoted earlier in this chapter. Tahera, who lives in Los Angeles, said: 'As Afghans we never felt close relationships with Arabs and Arab culture, especially after Bin Laden, who is from Saudi Arabia. But what is happening in Iraq and Palestine is an insult to all Muslims and people of Islamic culture. So we now feel close to them, more than ever before.' Islamophobia has triggered the trauma of displacement and the hostilities against them have greatly influenced their identities. Nasira described her experience:

> I feel a great deal of insult to my culture. I try to deal with anti-Muslim sentiments by educating my friends and talking to them; sometimes it is very difficult as I feel that they don't listen and they don't want to understand. But when they do listen and understand I feel that I have achieved a great deal. I try to convince my British friends that what the media says about Afghans and Muslims is not true.

Rahima also blames the American media for creating Islamophobia. She finds the internet a more useful and positive source of information:

> The white Americans who are in a minority in our area are very ignorant and they get their ideas from the media, especially the TV. I don't watch TV. I read newspapers. I read the *Los Angeles*

> *Times*, it is very biased, but it is better than the TV and other papers, especially on Palestine, Iraq and Afghanistan. I also get my ideas from the internet. By searching the internet I understand how biased the American media are. I compare them and I try to educate my friends and people around me.

Bas Gul was two years old when she settled in Los Angeles with her parents. When she was describing her experiences of post-9/11 she used the terms 'us' and 'them' interchangeably, to explain her Afghan/American identities. She said:

> When I was at school, most of my friends were white Americans. But now I go to university and most of my friends are from different ethnic groups and are more open-minded. I have been brought up as being outspoken and proud of my Afghan culture so no one ever dares to tease me or belittle me. Since 9/11 every now and then someone may say things like 'let us bomb them all'. I get very upset but I tell myself, these are the ignorant ones who should be left to rot in their ignorant life.

But her fear is that ignorance and the decline of rational thinking have resulted in wars and destruction. She continued:

> It is like *our president*. He is just totally ignorant; no one is able to convince him of anything. I am not anti-American. I know that in Afghanistan and those parts of the world there are also very ignorant people, like him. But, this is not an excuse that he goes and bombs *my country*. The younger generations in Iran and Pakistan have found integration into the exile system more difficult than did their parents' generation. Many feel far removed from either culture and they have to juggle two conflicting cultures which are too painful for them to cope with. The Afghans in the UK and the USA also feel the same way. However, there is an important difference, the tensions between the West and Islam, American, British and Afghan

cultures have created a world apart between them and these diasporic societies. Within Islamic culture in Iran and Pakistan they are able to find a space to struggle against their oppression and alienation. In the UK and the USA, for many the survival strategy is to close their doors to the physical and cultural hostilities since 9/11 and 7/7.

Tajbanoo has lived in Los Angeles for eighteen years. She practises Islam very strictly. She commented: 'During the month of Ramadan, I spend all my time in the mosque till late in the evening. I respect all other cultures and religions. But I keep to my own culture. After 9/11, they told me that if I continue to wear the *hijab* and go to the mosque they may kill me, I said fine, I will be proud to die in my *chaddari.*'

Suhaila said:

> My children were born in Afghanistan but they were brought up here in Los Angeles. My son sees himself more American than Afghan. My daughter sees herself as more Afghan than American. For me it is important that our children relate to Afghan culture and language. But the two cultures are a world apart. My children and other young Afghans say that we are Afghan at home and we are American outside of the home. But I know this is very hard for them. I am worried because I feel that our children are lost and confused.

Afghan young men from upper- and middle-class backgrounds living in the West are particularly under pressure by their fathers to carry on the culture of male domination. Abdulsatar, living in a white middle-class area of Los Angeles, explains how he finds the pressure of being Afghan, Muslim and American unbearable:

> As a child, I could not understand why the majority of the white Americans living in our neighbourhood were so racist towards us. My parents tried to prove that they are Americans, more than any other Afghans, as there is less nationalism

> and traditionalism in our household in comparison with my Afghan friends and the extended family. When I was fourteen I decided to be American. Suddenly my parents, especially my father, panicked and started saying that we are Afghans. They did not allow me to do the things that my American friends did. I felt lost and alienated and left home.

I found Afghan men, especially the older generation, in the West more patriarchal than Afghan men in Iran and Pakistan. Within an Islamic context, Afghan men in Iran and Pakistan are more open to new ideas. On the one hand they are under the pressure of material circumstances and, on the other hand, women are constantly struggling for change. As a result, they have no choice but to accept women's rights. Therefore, it is easier for Afghan women in Pakistan and Iran to cross the gender line within Islamic culture than for Afghan women in the UK and the USA.

The experiences of the younger generations raised in the West are also different from those of their counterparts in Iran and Pakistan where, in the context of Islamic culture, the first generation of Afghan women perceived themselves as cultural guardians, able to hold their communities together. The younger generation's hope for a better Afghanistan is based upon the image of the country drawn for them by the first generation. Their nomadic lifestyle has led to the realization that their identity is multiple and incorporates their past history, the diversity of their culture and the contradictions of their life in exile. They therefore try to synthesize the past and the present to build bridges between different generations, ethnicities and religions in order to ensure a better future.

The younger generation in the UK and the USA have responded differently to the hostility shown to Islamic culture, according to their class and the degree of flexibility in their family norms. This has determined whether their attitudes clash with those of their parents or they embrace the family's traditional values. Feelings of exile lead some to try very hard to integrate with their host societies, but this has generated dilemmas and uncertainties for them. Sherifa said:

> Most Afghan young people lead a double life. Most Afghan girls have non-Afghan boyfriends. They have to pretend around the family that they don't, because they are not allowed. But at the end of the day they go along with the traditional Afghan way of life. My parents don't force me to pray, but I am not allowed to take my boyfriend home. My brother is the same, he has a girlfriend but he does not talk about it either.

Her friend Sparghai has similar experiences: 'My parents do not want to know that I have a boyfriend so we don't talk about it. Therefore, like most Afghan young people, I also live a double life.' One mother said:

> My daughter told me that her American friends take their boyfriends/girlfriends home and introduce them to their families. I told my daughter that I cannot accept this norm. But I can accept that she sees her boyfriend behind my back. This is because I cannot stop her. We keep telling our children, virginity is important, you are not American, you are Afghan and so on. Therefore, there are cultural conflicts within our household. But we try to resolve it somehow. I feel that most of our children may take 5 per cent of what we try to teach them. But this 5 per cent is important and I will be very happy if they apply this 5 per cent when they are older.

Many practising Muslim women have rebelled against the popular western notion of sexual liberation and have embraced traditional Afghan mores. Halima said: 'I do not date. I do not feel that I am missing anything because all my American friends are unhappy about dating, they cry for being rejected, they don't really enjoy dating, so what is the point.' Rahima, from London, similarly said: 'I don't want to have a boyfriend. I don't want to go to nightclubs and parties. Sometimes I feel that I am missing something. But I love Afghan culture and our extended family gatherings and parties. I really enjoy them. So I don't want to spoil that.' Most of these young Afghans, in response to the clash of cultures, have isolated themselves from the wider society. In Los Angeles they speak English with a Los Angeles accent and do not have a grasp of Afghanistan as their country. Yet they still insisted on saying, 'I am Afghan.' Similarly, sixteen-year-old Setara, who speaks English with a London accent, says:

> I was born in London and I have never been to Afghanistan. But I feel 90 per cent Afghan and only 10 British. This is because I love Afghan culture and I have been brought up with it. I don't mind the white British way of life, but I prefer the Afghan way of life. I sometimes dislike it when my parents don't let me go out with my British friends. But I don't mind, because I go out with my Afghan and British Asian friends and with the extended family and enjoy it thoroughly.

The cultural pressures on Afghan communities in the UK and USA have forced many young Afghans to choose the respect, discipline and the closeness of Afghan extended family relations. The extended family sometimes imposes certain rules on young women. Some go along but others resist. Rahima stood up against the family pressure for wearing the *hijab*:

> My religion is very important for me, I pray and I fast throughout the month of Ramadan, but I don't wear the *hijab*. It is my decision. My mother and my extended family would prefer it if I wore it, but I argued with them that Islam is about judging a person for what she/he is and not what they wear. It is difficult to go to school with *hijab*, so I don't wear it. I have convinced my family and now they are OK with what I want.

These women's stories suggest that the extended family, though supportive, is itself not free from various painful forms of conflict, but, in the face of Islamophobia, many women chose to devote their lives to looking after the children and teenagers within their extended family. Rahima felt that the younger generation could not relate to the older members of the family because they are too conservative, but they could relate to her more than to their own parents. She, therefore, has devoted her life to these young people. When they face dilemmas, contradictions and cultural conflicts, she understands them. She speaks English well; she goes to their schools and sorts out their problems for them. She says: 'I have chosen this role. For me this is like doing community work. If I don't do this there will be many conflicts between different generations within the extended family and the community.'

Despite being caught between the conservatism of families and the hostility of the exile societies, many young Afghans hope for a better future for their children. Fatima said:

> I will bring up my children differently to the way that my mother brought me up, I don't want them to be Americanized. I want them to be Afghans but with more power of decision making. I want them to be able to decide for themselves, I want them to have more power than I had. I think both cultures have good and bad sides to them. My aim is to grab the good sides of both cultures.

Nargis had a similar view: 'I will bring up my little boy the Afghan way: that is, respecting parents, family and teachers. The sort of things most children in British society do not respect. I want him to speak Dari, at the same time; I want him to be able to decide for himself and learn to be independent.'

The identities and cultural experiences of Afghan women and men in the West are also influenced by African American, Asian, Middle Eastern and Latin American cultural styles as well as white Britain and white America. They try to interpret certain aspects of their lives according to these cultures. Their mutual isolation, alienation and suffering, although diverse and complex, give them a sense of power and solidarity with each other. In London and Los Angeles in particular, many feel that they are one of many in the melting pot of immigrant identity. Suhaila states:

> Since 9/11 we feel a great deal of racism against us. Nevertheless, because American society is a melting pot, it is possible to survive more easily. We try to relate to other immigrant communities. Our home is Afghanistan, but because in America everybody is an immigrant, in a strange way sometimes we feel this can be home for us, as we are all outsiders.

Nevertheless, in the USA, anti-Muslim sentiment has become so strong that non-white immigrant communities also have been hostile to Afghans and Muslims. Despite feelings of solidarity with Palestinian and Iraqis, there are certainly divisions within the Muslim communities. Young Afghans have found these divisions painful as it has added to their sense of being *sargardan* (wanderers). Saffiullah said: 'I think that Islam can unify us. But the problem is that we see each other as the Other. As Afghans, Iranians, Arabs, Turks, Egyptians and so on, we have different mosques and there is a lot of finger pointing among us. But the enemy sees us all as Muslims. So we should unite as Muslims and defend each other against the common enemy.'

Najia from London feels that the divisiveness has made her understand that identity is something that changes all the time: 'In search of my identity one time I was Muslim, one time I was reading Persian literature. Then I decided to stop searching and make peace with my diverse Afghan identity made up of all different things.' Others have realized that their relationship with the rest of the world cannot be based on isolated Muslim immigrant communities; they have to rebuild their world by sharing different aspects of their varied lives. Saffiullah succeeded in doing this: 'In order to survive, I had to do something. I spoke with some of my African American, Afghan and Iranian friends. We put together a music group and we produce anti-war rap music on CD.' Others have tried to create an

Afghan/Muslim/British/American identity which represents the link between the outsider and the insider. As Zalmai argued: 'To isolate oneself from other cultures and move from one extreme to another extreme is alienating and dangerous.' Young Afghan women who are not practising Muslims and do not wear the *hijab* try to combine different aspects of their Afghan Muslim western culture, but sometimes they feel rejected by both sides. Malalai said: 'I feel that I am both American and Afghan. But when I am with Americans I don't feel totally American. When I am at home, I don't feel totally Afghan. With Americans I feel that I have to defend my Afghan culture. With Afghans I feel that because I dress like Americans, they don't really like me and they don't embrace me as they should do. But I try to be both, no matter how hard it is.' Saghar tries to rise above the contradictions:

> To Afghans I am American and to Americans I am Afghan. Sometimes I feel this is beautiful as I can step outside of one and enter the other. I can step outside of American culture and criticize it and vice versa. I feel that Americans are so blind with their arrogance that they cannot see any criticisms of their culture. The same with Afghans. They are so arrogant with their culture that they cannot see any criticisms of themselves. I went through hell to arrive where I am now. I am now happy with what I am.

In the UK, Afghan women's lives have become increasingly confined to resisting Islamophobia and stereotypical representations. They have felt rejected by the West's condemnation of their culture and constantly feel the need to be on the defensive. They have very little space in which to struggle for their gender rights. They feel a political divide between themselves and western feminists, believing that for many years western feminists ignored the suffering of Afghan women as their governments supported the Mujaheddin, Bin Laden and the Taliban. Under pressure from Afghan women, as late as 1997, the Feminist Majority Foundation in the USA campaigned to change US foreign policy and that of the UN to non-recognition of the Taliban by lobbying the Clinton administration. But neither Clinton nor Bush demonstrated any concern for Afghan women until after 9/11 when they used the rhetoric of women's rights to gain support for the war. Eleanor Smeal, leader of the Feminist Majority Foundation, supported the war and cheered American and other western women in every level of the army on their way 'to liberate Afghan women from their *Borqa*'.[34] Ferida described the situation:

> We set up our own women's organizations to work with Afghan women. We tried to discuss with the representatives of the US government, the UN and the feminist groups about Afghanistan and women's issues. However, all they were interested in was the issue of *chaddari* (*burqa*). But for us that is not an issue. For us if women have access to education, health and employment it does not matter what they wear. After they attacked Afghanistan they brought a large number of *burqa*s from Afghanistan, they cut the part where Afghan women wear it on their head and in front of their eyes and they sold it in their meetings in the name of women's liberation in Afghanistan. I was hurt by it; many Afghan friends were hurt by it. It was an insult to Afghan women. I felt that they don't understand our culture and they have their own agenda. In my view, women can wear *chaddari* but also have education and access to employment. Now that Afghanistan is in their hands, they don't talk about why women resort to self-burning and why women still do not have access to health, education and employment.

In their attempts to rout the Taliban and al-Qaida, the Bush and Blair administrations have portrayed the war against Afghanistan as a humanitarian war to protect the Afghan people. Women are appointed to high political and military[35] positions; the language of women's rights is used to justify their imperialist agenda.[36] Afghan women are portrayed as the ultimate victims of the Taliban and the USA as their ultimate protector. Iris Young argues that the same feminists who criticized the practice of male protection of women in Muslim majority societies as masculinism and patriarchal fell into the trap of 'masculinist protection' as practised by Bush and Blair (good men protecting them from bad men attacking them). They even submitted to their rules and decisions without criticizing them for curtailing civil liberties.[37]

Volumes have been written about feminism, war and the military.[38] But western feminism, as a movement and as a force, has failed to participate in the international peace movements or to stop the US policy of control of the Middle East and Central Asia. Afghan women feel that what is happening in Afghanistan has not been of concern to western feminists. As Stanley and Wise have argued, feminism in the West has become simply an academic and intellectual, rather than a practical political, concern.[39] Thus, Afghan women do not see themselves as part of the western feminist movement. They feel excluded by feminists, more so in the USA than in the UK, because of the failure to construct a more inclusive feminism that embraces all ethnicities, nations, religions and cultures.[40]

As do women in Iran and Pakistan, Afghan women in the UK and the USA define gender relations sometimes in terms of greater equality and sometimes in terms of their own understanding of concepts of community and continuity. The important difference, however, is that the more they are forced to live on the margins of British and American societies, the more they become determined to hang on to traditional gender roles. Palwasha commented: 'We are too hard on ourselves, our men and our societies. In fact, in some ways, women are respected much more in our Islamic societies and by our own men than in these western societies and by western men.'

These women are fully aware of the repressive gender bias in their own cultures, but they object to western feminists who see men as enemies.[41] Rahima argued: 'In most cases women are not treated as equals to men within the Afghan communities. We will have to change that, but we need to educate our women and men. We must become convinced of the fact that women, men and children will benefit from gender equality, to exclude is divisive and against our culture.'

Young Afghan women born in the USA or UK and those who settled there at a very young age were teenagers at the time of 9/11. For them, subsequent events have been deeply alienating. Where conservative gender roles are imposed on them, most do not rebel because the close community and family, even with all their problems and contradictions, are safer for them than being an outsider in the wider hostile society. As Maliha argued: 'The problems of being inside are more bearable than facing the problems outside.' Tahera also confirmed that: 'The love, comfort and the affection of the traditional way of life within the family and the extended family is comforting and the rejection in the wider society is painful. So we have made a choice.'

Yet, despite their alienation, many of these young Afghans hope for a better future. Setara said: 'Young Afghans in the USA have reinterpreted the concept of the "American dream" according to their own experiences and hope for the future.' Farzana said: 'I want to be a judge; this is the most important thing in my life. I don't want to go back to Afghanistan now, maybe later; I'd like to be able to defend the rights of Middle Easterners and Afghans and Muslims in the USA.' Nazia also described her wishes: 'I don't think I am big enough to go and change people. I feel I can help by being a good Afghan American and a good Muslim, this way I can help. I feel that I am all three of them, Afghan, American, Muslim. I want to use the good education system here and make a lot of money and then go and help Afghanistan.' Aymal, a young Pashtun man in Los Angeles, said: 'I was born in the USA. But as an Afghan and Muslim, they see me as a threat and enemy. I fear that if another incident like 9/11 happens they will put us all in concentration camps. So I see this country as a land of opportunity for only a certain kind of people and not for all Americans. I don't belong here. I want to go to Afghanistan and help to rebuild it.'

Conclusion

Experiences of the trauma of displacement, confusion over identity, loss of status, facing racism and a life of marginalization unite all Afghan women in the diaspora. Similarly, the first generation of Afghan women in all these societies try to pass their heritage on to the younger generations. The differences in the experiences of Afghan women and men in the UK and the USA compared with those in Iran and Pakistan are striking. In the UK and the USA, the transition to exile is particularly affected by their class position in Afghanistan. Despite economic, social and racial exclusion, many Afghans, especially in Iran, have benefited from education and do not want to go back to Afghanistan. In the UK and the USA, however, their highly educated and high social status in Afghanistan in the past is in stark contrast to the racism and loss of status that they face. The impact of 9/11 and 7/7 on their lives is overwhelming. They feel isolated and threatened.

In Iran and Pakistan there is a general desire for fuller integration. In the UK and the USA, the younger generation is under enormous pressure from Islamophobia and the tension created by the media and the politicians. They feel isolated and alienated and are reluctant to integrate. Their struggle and resistance are concentrated on combating western stereotypes of Afghans and Muslims. Some try to tear down the western walls in order to be accepted as an integral part of western culture. Others build more walls as they find the rejection of living in exile on the margins of established norms unbearable. Some resort to creating a false identity and denying their own marginality in order to adhere to accepted norms of western culture. Others try to hang on to their marginality and Afghan culture. The majority, however, try to create an Afghan/Muslim/British/American identity which represents the link between the outsider and the insider. For women in Pakistan and Afghanistan, and for the majority of women in Iran, the concept of feminism is based on their understanding of identity. Many include on their agenda the emancipation of children and men in the context of social power. In the West they are aware of a political divide between themselves and the western feminists. They challenge the concept of a universal experience of oppression.

Afghan women in Iran and Pakistan have more in common with Pakistani and Iranian women than Afghan women have with American and British women. The former are better equipped to struggle for their gender rights and resist a hostile environment. Afghan women in the West do not have this space in which to struggle for their gender rights. Afghan women in Iran and Pakistan appreciate a level of individualism. In contrast, Afghan women in the West feel that too much individualism is in contradiction to their cultural identity. Many Afghan men in these societies do not find a contradiction between their traditional gender ideology and women's rights to education, healthcare and employment. But in the UK and the USA, under pressure of anti-Muslim sentiments, they have a tendency to hang on to their male authority and to impose on women the traditional Afghan gender relations. Nevertheless, Afghan women in diasporic communities are optimistic. What they share, despite their differences, is a desire to free themselves from all kinds of constraints and build a better future.

Notes

1 UNHCR 2003 and 2004.

2 Rajaee 2000: 59; and Abbasi-Shavazi et al. 2005a: iii; and AREU 2005c.

3 AREU 2005a: 1.

4 AREU 2006a.

5 Ibid. and AREU 2005b.

6 Abbasi-Shavazi et al. 2005a: 11; and AREU 2006a and 2005b.

7 Security and Development Policy Group 2006: 7: www.senliscouncil.net

8 Sadr 2002: 16–18; and Ebrahimi 2004a and 2004b: 9–10 and 2002: 24–7.

9 Abbasi-Shavazi et al. 2005a, 2005b and 2005c.

10 Monsutti 2004: 219–40;

Phizacklea 2003; Alberts 2003: 285–98; Vertovec 1999: 447–62; Portes 1997: 812 and 799–825.

11 For details of Afghans' status in Iran, see also ILO 2006.

12 AREU 2005a: 26–8; and AREU 2006b: 28–33.

13 *The Afghan Alphabet* and *Baran* by Mohsen Makhmalbaf; *At Five in the Afternoon* by Samira Makhmalbaf; and *Stray Dogs* by Marzieh Meshkini.

14 AREU 2005a: 29–30.

15 Erel et al. 2003: 264; Turner 1993; Lenz et al. 2002: 8; Phoenix 1998: 67 and 859–80.

16 I use the term Islamic culture to mean people who live in Muslim majority societies who may be of different faith or no faith but who nevertheless 'carry' the dominant Islamic culture.

17 For this discussion, see Moser and Clark 2001: 9–10.

18. This was also noted by Abbasi-Shavazi et al. 2005a, 2005b, 2005c; and AREU 2006a.

19 For this discussion, see also Orlando 1999: 164.

20 For an excellent analysis of diasporic identities, see Orlando 1999.

21 Said 1996: 61.

22 In formulating my analysis of Afghan women, I was greatly influenced by Orlando's discussion on this subject. See Orlando 1999: 167.

23 For similar experiences, see Stewart and Strathern 2000: 277.

24 This Shi'a tradition is practised in some parts of Iran and among some old-fashioned traditional communities. It is similar to burning an effigy of Guy Fawkes in the UK. Omar was one of the Sunni leaders of early Islam who defeated the Shi'a leadership.

25 Rostami-Povey 2001 and 2004c or 2004d and 2005.

26 See Poya 1999; and Iran Statistical Centre 2006.

27. This tradition was quite common in Iran, see Poya 1999: 87–9.

28 For similar findings, see Hoodfar 2004.

29 Shah 2000: 106–7.

30 Hagopian 2004; Haddad 2006.

31 Ahmed 1992.

32 This phrase has repeatedly been used by the western media.

33 Ahmed 1999; and McDonald 2006.

34 Young 2003.

35. Flanders 2004.

36 Eisenstein 2004.

37 Young 2003. For criticisms of western feminism before 9/11, see Mohanty 1991; Ahmed 1992; Narayan 1997, among others. Post-9/11 and -7/7, this position re-emerged as part of the discourse of Islamophobia to justify wars. For this discussion, see Abu-Lughod 2002; and Bahramitash 2005: 223–37, among others.

38 Elshtain 1995; Tickner 2001; Enloe 2004; Cockburn 2003; Jones 2003.

39 Stanley and Wise 2000: 261–88.

40 Young 2003: 1–25; Lutz 2002; Stanley and Wise 2000 provide an excellent discussion on this issue.

41 For similar arguments, see Matsuoka and Sorenson 2003: 219–41.

5 | Challenging domination

> 'Women's rights and democracy cannot be imported to Afghanistan. We have to do it according to our Afghan norms and values, otherwise they will lose their meanings.' Hamasa, Jalalabad

It is only by listening to Afghan women's and men's voices that we can begin to understand their struggle for their identity, rights and recognition. This book has tried to present the world, in particular the international events which have enveloped Afghanistan, from their point of view. Afghan women have too often been spoken for and represented by the media, politicians and academics in the West. Here, they speak for themselves. They want all those people who hope for gender equality, peace, security and development in Afghanistan to know that they are able to struggle against local male domination in their own way and according to their culture. The roots of patriarchal oppression go deep in Afghan society – far deeper than the Taliban or al-Qaida. The western perception that women's liberation will come with liberation from these forces is simplistic at best and damaging at worst.

Male dominance and female subordination in Afghanistan can be traced back to pre-Islamic civilizations in the region when male dominance and the patriarchal family were entrenched through the rise of urban class societies and increasing military competition. Islam inherited and reconstituted the social organization of gender in pre-Islamic civilizations.[1] Since the expansion of the Islamic empire in the region, Afghanistan reformulated gender power relations, according to ethnic diversity, internal socio-economic changes and external influences. Customs and formulas determining the control and exclusion of women have been reshaped and renegotiated with historical change.

Acknowledging existing patriarchal attitudes and structures requires us to recognize the diversity of male attitudes and actions, and to admit that while some men resist gender equality, others respond positively to women's demands. As much as there is conflict between men and women, there is harmony and solidarity between them and family and community are important parts of their lives. Afghan women and men are able to determine the course of their lives but they insist on doing this according to their own cultures and religions. Advocating respect for people's culture is not a recourse to cultural relativism or identity politics. It is also not to reduce the complex politics, social dynamics and diversity of Afghan people to their religion. It is about the importance of Afghan Islamic culture, a core part of their history, personal and political identity that they feel is under attack by the invading forces. It is about being deprived of healthcare, education and employment, which takes away their agency and ability to change their society and the gender power relations within it.

Afghan women's and men's perception of women's liberation is a world apart from that of the invading forces. The western perception of women's liberation and democracy wrongly advocates that Afghan women and men should simply abandon the repressive practices of their culture and adopt the 'superior' western culture. Today, Washington's and London's agenda is similar to the old imperial agenda. They use the same thesis of western superiority to serve their domination of Afghanistan as an important part of their plan for reshaping the Middle East and Central Asia. However, their typical imperial strategy, which was doomed to failure in the past, is now doomed to fail in Afghanistan. The US, NATO and ISAF forces, with their military might, cannot force women's liberation and democracy on Afghan women and men. This does not mean that Afghanistan as an Islamic country is unchangeable, or that

Afghan women and men are locked into their past, incapable of change. As shown in Chapter 3, the same men who have allowed their daughters to go to school, university and to work in Iran and Pakistan, attempt to lock women inside the home back in Afghanistan.

For Afghan women, the western imperial account of their oppression is based on misrepresentation and political manipulation. The history of Afghan women's resistance and struggles against the injustices of their indigenous cultures is rich. As we have seen in this book, during the period of the civil war (1992–96), sexual violence against women escalated to an unprecedented level. The Taliban rule sought the solution in drastically restricting women's movements in order to put a stop to them being raped and/or engaging in sex work. The Taliban persecuted women for the violation of its rules, but women courageously and imaginatively resisted those restrictive social norms. Women of diverse ethnic and religious groups worked together through their secret schools. Their activities laid the foundation for the building of social capital; by creating networks of trust and reciprocity they gave cohesion to their communities and had great hopes for the future.

After the fall of the Taliban, they believed that, in their own way and according to their own culture, they could change their communities to accept women's participation in the economy and society and find legitimate roles for women in the process of reconstruction. However, under NATO rule, the change in their material conditions that would prefigure such social transformation is absent. Their country has been left shattered and fragmented. The brutal rule of the Taliban has been replaced by the brutal rule of warlords. This is a desperate reminder that before the Taliban, the rule of the warlords led to a horrifying civil war to which Afghans saw the Taliban as the solution. Alien regimes from the British rule to Russian, Taliban and now the USA, ISAF and NATO, have no legitimacy in Afghanistan. The state is legitimate only if it ensures the independence of

Afghanistan, if it respects Islamic values, if it acts as a broker between different ethnic groups and provides security and access to health, education and employment.[2] The present state in Afghanistan has subjugated the needs of the majority of the people to the imperial interests of the USA. The state has failed to bring about meaningful reconstruction and has facilitated an assault on Afghan religion and culture by the alien invaders. This state of affairs has invalidated both the legitimacy of the state and the West's principles of justice, liberation and democracy.

The system of governance that foreign invaders are extending to Afghanistan is not working to the advantage of the Afghan people. Their model of western economic and cultural imposition has created a corrupt world for Afghans that has deprived them of the material resources essential for transforming both gender relations and their society as a whole. They cannot tolerate the sort of modernity offered by the contemporary neoliberal politics and governance. All they see that they are being offered is inequality, cruelty and injustice.

Above all, the present system has destabilized and antagonized existing social relations, including gender relations. In the context of invasion, men and women are not motivated to seek more positive change. The absence of meaningful change in people's material conditions and the imposition of an alien culture have made Afghanistan and the Afghan people more conservative. For Afghan men, only two options have been available: being engaged in the fighting and becoming more aggressive, or failing to protect and provide for their family members, which they consider as an assault on their masculine identity. The more the alien forces are determined to pursue their onslaught on Afghan society, economy and culture, the more Afghans are determined to resist them. In this situation, social norms are hardening for women as they come under pressure to conform to the exclusionary norms of their communities.

This is the polarizing effect of the imposition of western

modernity. As we have seen in this book, the continuing conflict and lack of economic development and security intensify women's oppression. Even in Kabul and other urban centres, women are restricted. Images of shrouded women in the blue *chaddari* are a visible reminder of the way women are under pressure from both local males and imperial domination and so do not feel safe without it. Yet the *chaddari* is only the tip of the iceberg of male control over female bodies. Patriarchal family laws with regard to marriage, divorce, custody of children, forced marriages and honour killing and the denial of women's access to healthcare, education and employment are continuing.

Afghan women's vision of how to seek gender equality and what it means to them is crystal clear. As the women in this book constantly reiterated, the domination and oppression they face is as much imperial as patriarchal. In their view, socio-economic development, engaging all ethnic groups and religions, is the only way to achieve peace, security and development and this can pave the way for change in gender relations. However, instead of development, peace and security, the invaders use the concept of women's rights, human rights, democracy and humanitarian intervention to advocate imperial domination.[3]

Twenty-seven years of war and violent conflicts forced 7 million Afghans to leave their country. The multiplicity of women's stories in diaspora reveals the variety of their experiences according to ethnicity, religion, age, class, geographical positioning as well as their social-cultural milieu and socio-economic constraints. They have been subject to racism, but collectively remembering Afghanistan enables them to overcome their alienation. Their experiences of these diasporic communities have motivated them to develop a vision of rebuilding a better Afghanistan, Afghanistan as a nation. The ideology of the Iranian women's movement and the support that they have received from women's NGOs in Pakistan has enabled them to challenge male, ethnic, age and religious domination. In the

UK and the USA, however, they have been constantly engaged in mediating between and compromising 'western' values and their Afghan/Muslim cultural identity. Their lives are confined to constantly striving to challenge the West's view of Afghan Muslim women. Therefore, their engagement in this battle has overshadowed their struggle against male domination. In Iran and Pakistan they redefine gender relations towards greater equality. In the UK and USA, in the more alien culture in which they find themselves, they are more likely to maintain their traditional communal gender relations. In Iran and in Pakistan, within the Islamic context and culture, they have found a space to enrich their collective Afghan identity. In the UK and the USA, however, where they face systematic attacks on their Islamic culture and identity, they tend to hang on to their Muslim collective identity.

As women's voices in this book have repeatedly stressed, foreign domination and invasion have always had a negative impact on their identity and their struggle for rights and equality. Under the Russian invasion they lost faith in secularist ideology and 'communism'. After two decades of war and conflict, today they are facing western invasion of their country. Under these circumstances, the women's movement in Afghanistan can only use the idiom of religion to gain mass support and legitimacy.

Despite many obstacles on their path, women's rights activists in Afghanistan and in the diaspora believe that the conservative tradition of controlling and excluding women has no place in Afghanistan and Islamic culture. Since the late nineteenth century, a reformist tendency within the Muslim world, including Afghanistan, has emphasized women's education. Initially only a minority of intellectual women from the upper and middle classes benefited from educational opportunities, though in some Muslim societies these opportunities extended to the working classes.[4] This is the Islam that they identify with, an Islam that encourages the education of women and men.

Inspired by Afghanistan's history as a modern, Islamic country with a mixture of European and Asian influences and diverse cultures, they believe that it will be possible to achieve this in the twenty-first century.

Historically, feminism in Muslim majority societies has been diverse. Critical tensions have existed within feminist discourse ranging from affiliation to westernizing and secularizing tendencies to voices searching for a way to articulate women's rights and gender equality within an indigenous discourse, including Islamic discourse. My analysis of the Afghan women's movement demonstrates a critical consciousness of the politics of local male domination and a feminist contestation of the cultural practices sanctioning injustices to women. The dominant tendency suggests the reforming of the laws advocating the unjust treatment of women within the Afghan/Islamic context, and not abandoning their heritage.

However, this interpretation of Islam is far removed from that of the Taliban or al-Qaida. In this path they are not alone; there is a rich literature by Muslim and secular feminists who identify with Islamic culture. For decades they have discussed the positive side of Islamic culture and history. Haleh Afshar, Leila Ahmed, Riffat Hassan and Fatema Mernissi, among others, have discussed the history of powerful and respected women in Islam from Khadija, the first wife of the prophet Muhammad and first convert to Islam; to Aisha, the youngest and last wife of the prophet who is considered to convey the most reliable source of Islamic law.[5] They see Islamic marriage as a contract in which women's work is paid, valued and not invisible. Like the Afghan women discussed in this book, these scholars argue that Islam has given women more rights than any other religious tradition. They have criticized the conservative and patriarchal tradition in Islam which has taken away women's rights and continues to subject women to unequal treatment. At the same time they have challenged the perception of Muslim women in the West.[6] They have argued that the West's simplistic views of women's place in Islam are part of the context of narratives of inferiority and otherness. To advance its imperial domination, the West has conveniently ignored the achievements of women in Islamic societies throughout the twentieth century and until today.

Ziba Mir-Hosseini has provided a historical analysis of the different stages of women's struggle for change. She distinguishes between the 'traditionalist' approach, based on the discourse of the classical Shari'a texts, which in her view are the genesis of gender inequality, and the 'modernist' approach developed in the early part of the twentieth century, based on the modern legal systems inspired by western models in Muslim countries. Since then, she argues, the status of women has become a contested issue and has remained a battleground between the forces of 'traditionalism' and 'modernity' in the Muslim world. In the 1990s, a reformist trend emerged enabling women to achieve gender equality through reforming laws and regulations.[7] Throughout the late twentieth century and since the beginning of the twenty-first century, we have seen politicized Muslim women writing their own interpretations of their rights, and about their struggle to achieve these rights. They have argued systematically that there is no contradiction between fighting for gender rights and remaining good Muslims.[8] In this context, the experience of the women's rights movement in Iran is particularly important and relevant to Afghan women. They have challenged the hegemony of traditional interpretations of the Shari'a and have questioned the very legitimacy of state laws. At the beginning of the twenty-first century, women's rights are no longer a taboo subject as women demand solutions to gender inequalities within an Islamic context.[9]

As I have written elsewhere, the change in gender relations in Iran is closely related to material transformation. Since 1979 the Islamic state and other institutions have provided healthcare, education and employment to large sections of society that were previously marginalized and excluded by the pro-western secular regime of the 1960s and 1970s. Gender segregation, including the compulsory wearing of the *hijab*, was initially intended as a barrier to women's participation in society. For the majority of women, however, the Islamization of state and society removed the obstacles for the full participation in the social, economic and political spheres. The doors of schools and universities opened up to women wearing the *hijab*. In 2007, 64 per cent of university students are women. In this process, the material encountered the ideological and led to gender consciousness. Educated young women began to realize the limitations of the Islamic state and other institutions with regard to gender equality and began their struggle for change against traditional gender relations. The growing overlap and unity between secular and religious women has produced reforms in family law, education and employment regulations which have favoured women.[10] Millions of Afghan women living in Iran for twenty-five years have experienced the success of Iranian women in advocating policies and cultures of women's rights as well as secularism and pluralism. They have witnessed how women in a Muslim majority society have been standing for the adoption and protection of the full range of human rights; for equality under law and for equal protection from the power of the state and conservative religious forces. Moreover, they have achieved a great deal, although there is still a long way to go. In a nutshell, the success of the Iranian women's movement is a result of improvement in their material conditions and its grassroots origins, two important issues which have consistently been denied in Afghanistan, where institutions have for so long been imposed from above and outside.

The imperial agenda

The implications of reactions to current practice in Afghanistan and the Middle East demand far more attention from western feminists, who have argued that feminist consciousness and feminist social practices are crucial resources in the fight against violence, war and conflict. The invasion of Afghanistan was facilitated by the rhetoric of gender equality and women's rights and since the invasion these issues have been manipulated by both government and NGOs and by gender experts who are able to present an image of the Afghan government and international institutions as committed to women's rights. As I have discussed in this book, there can be no doubt that the Afghan women who are engaged with women's issues within the government and the parliament, the UN organizations and some international NGOs are genuinely committed to gender equality. However, women's rights issues have become depoliticized and have been hijacked by government and international financial institutions. Special government funds and programmes have been set up to incorporate women into peace building and conflict resolution. Different UN organizations and NGOs are competing with each other over gender mainstreaming and gender integration into economic and political processes. In this context, everybody and everything responsible for gender equality in Afghanistan equates to nobody and nothing being responsible for putting women's interests and experiences of injustice on the political agenda.

As was discussed earlier, the manipulation of women's rights has existed for a long time. The British in India and Egypt, the French in Algeria and at present America in the Middle East and Afghanistan have all used the notion of 'saving women' in these societies to gain support for their colonial and imperial projects. In Victorian England, the colonial establishment hijacked the language of feminism to justify the western domination of Islamic societies. In her groundbreaking book, *Women and Gender in Islam*,[11] Leila Ahmed discusses in detail how the natural female inferiority and domesticity were advocated and vaunted as ideals in Victorian England. In the empire, however, the rhetoric of 'liberating' Muslim women from Muslim men's 'oppression' was used hypocritically to legitimize western superiority and attack Islamic culture and heritage. They co-opted the discourses of western superiority and domination within the ideology of feminism. They perceived the veil and segregation as the epitome of Muslim women's oppression and the inferiority of Islamic societies. Based on this imperial feminism, they promoted the idea that Muslim women would be liberated by adopting western culture and way of life.

Throughout the nineteenth and twentieth centuries and until today, the history of Afghanistan, and indeed the histories of all Muslim majority societies, demonstrate that whenever the imperial powers adopted the rhetoric of women's liberation in order to justify their imperial domination, they faced resistance and rejection. 'Saving Muslim women' was and still is a typical imperial strategy. It is for this reason that in Muslim majority societies feminist ideology and women's rights movements have historically been associated with nationalism, anti-colonialism and anti-imperialism.[12] As Afghan women have emphasized in this book, the form of feminism that they identify with is within Islamic culture, the rights and roles of women in Islam and how in this context they are looking for emancipation in their daily lives.

Today, in a similar way to the colonial era and with few exceptions, western feminists do not challenge the imperial agenda and do not perceive its relationship to their own feminism. They do not attempt to understand women in Muslim societies, especially Afghan women; they do not challenge the deployment of feminism against Islamic cultures and the use of feminist ideology as a tool serving the US-led military domination in Afghanistan and the region.

A pyramid of female power has been created which includes presidential advisers, members of cabinets, parliaments, senates and other powerful institutions. Their numbers may be fewer than men, but they are effectively in support of the wars and ignore the suffering of millions of women, men and children in Afghanistan and the region. The mobilization of western women across class and ethnicity into the right-wing politics of war and violent conflict – ranging from the role played by Condoleezza Rice and other neo-conservative women in the Bush administration to female soldiers participating in killing and abusing people in Afghanistan, Iraq and elsewhere – has discredited the idea that if more women were in positions of power, they would change the violent nature of wars and strengthen the peacemaking processes. The implications of this for our understandings of feminism and war are wide-ranging.

Women in the Muslim majority societies and women of Islamic culture in the West have been disheartened by the way in which women's oppression has been used to promote war and conflict in Afghanistan and the Middle East. Mistrust of western feminism in Afghanistan now runs deep. Lila Abu-Lughod has argued that the 'very strong appeal' of the notion of 'saving Afghan women' justifies American intervention in Afghanistan and that dampens criticisms of intervention by American and European feminists. The hypocritical feminism of the Republican administration reinforces a western sense of superiority.[13]

Western feminism has gained academic legitimacy. However, feminists' largely passive stance against neo-liberalism and the erosion of the welfare state has meant the deterioration of the lives of millions of poorer women and women of colour in the West and throughout the world. As violence against women, sexism and the persistence of conventional gender relations continue, powerful governments and financial and military institutions co-opt the rhetoric and the language of feminism. These concepts are redefined to imply that the West, especially the USA, is civilized while other civilizations border on barbarism. These issues have been manipulated with considerable success and have become tools to mask global misogynist practices and to justify war and imperial domination.[14]

Today, Afghan women and women throughout the Muslim majority societies and elsewhere are actively engaged critically and constructively with the oppressive practices in their own cultures, in their own terms. From North Africa to South East Asia, the parliaments in these Muslim majority societies are debating women's issues and democracy. Without compromising national and different forms of Islamic heritages, women have been standing strong against Islamist men who have denounced feminism as western. They are resisting the East–West, tradition–modernity, Islamic–sinful dichotomies and have tried to be engaged with the dynamics of the encounter of their culture and feminism in the West.[15] They have been learning from the positive contribution of western feminisms and have passionately adopted the commitment to enable women to develop their full potential to struggle for gender equality. Their strength is in their ability to cross the boundaries of different forms of feminism to find a commonality between women's global concerns and their own local needs.

Today, western feminism can benefit from Afghan women's critical adaptation of the ideas of individualism and the values of westernization which are not unambiguously beneficial. As discussed in Chapter 4, Afghan women in the USA were critical of the Feminist Majority Foundation and became suspicious of their support. These American feminists, instead of understanding Afghan women's struggle and culture, easily fell into the trap of the idea that Islamic culture is incompatible with western principles of egalitarian thought, especially in the context of gender equality and democracy. Based on this theory, they used Afghan women's criticisms of their own local patriarchal structures to portray Afghan and Islamic culture as inferior to western culture, and later they used this perceived inferiority to justify the participation of western women in the invasion of Afghanistan. They devalued Afghan culture by presuming that the only way for Afghan women's liberation is to adopt the western model. Therefore, Afghan women have found western feminism to be elitist, imperialist and disconnected from the reality of their lives.

Feminism is incredibly diverse, incorporating numerous

perspectives and areas of concern. Western feminisms need to step away from the imperial agenda and incorporate the views of Afghan women, women of Islamic culture and indeed other cultures, to become broader, more inclusive, and ultimately a stronger force for change. Afghan women's voices are important for what is traditionally understood as feminism. Feminist rhetoric used to justify invasion has led to a near-wholesale rejection of feminism in Afghanistan and has had a polarizing effect. The Muslim and western conceptions of feminism and women's rights need to intermingle and learn from one another, to construct a more inclusive, global vision of feminism that people can use to struggle for their rights in the context of their own identities and communities. Afghan women have spoken, they are very brave and their demands are very clear. We can only hope that their voices and their energy will be strong enough to overcome all kinds of domination and to construct a better future for the twenty-first century.

Notes

1 Ahmed 1992: 39–124.

2 Johnson and Leslie 2004: 138.

3 For this discussion, see Kerr et al. 2004: 190; and Islam and Hassan 2004: 201–13.

4 Ahmed 1992: 169–88; Poya 1999: 94–120.

5 See Afshar 2005: www.royalphil.arts.gla.ac.uk; Ahmed 1992: 41–78; Hassan, 'Religious Conservatism': www.irfi.org/article_101_150/religious_conservatism.htm; and 'Religious Consultation': www.religiousconsultation.org/hassan.htm

6 See Abu-Lughod 2002; 2006: www.asiasource.org/news/special_reports/lila.cfm; 1998 and 1999; Afshar et al. 2005: 268–73; and 2006; Ahmed 1992; Hassan 2002; Mernissi 2002, 2001 and 1997.

7 Mir-Hosseini 2003: www.brill.nl; and 2002 and 2006; see also Ebadi 2006.

8 Afshar et al. 2005: 268–73.

9 Mir-Hosseini 2002.

10 Poya 1999.

11 Ahmed 1999.

12 Eisenstein 2004: 148–80 and Al-Ali 2003.

13 See Asia Source interview with Lila Abu-Lughod: www.asiasource.org/news/special_reports/lila.cfm

14 See Ackerly and D'Costa 2005.

15 Abu-Lughod 1998: 13–22.

Bibliography

Abbasi-Shavazi, M. J. et al. (2005a) 'Return to Afghanistan? A Study of Afghans Living in Mashhad, Islamic Republic of Iran', Kabul: AREU (Afghan Research and Evaluation Unit).

— (2005b) 'Return to Afghanistan? A Study of Afghans Living in Zahedan, Islamic Republic of Iran', Kabul: AREU (Afghan Research and Evaluation Unit).

— (2005c) 'Return to Afghanistan? A Study of Afghans Living in Tehran, Islamic Republic of Iran', Kabul: AREU (Afghan Research and Evaluation Unit).

Abu-Lughod, L. (ed.) (1998) *Remaking Women, Feminism and Modernity in the Middle East*, Princeton, NJ: Princeton University Press.

— (1999) *Veiled Sentiments, Honor and Poetry in a Bedouin Society*, Berkeley, Los Angeles and London: University of California Press.

— (2002) 'Do Muslim Women Really Need Saving? Anthropological Reflections on Cultural Relativism and Its Others', *American Anthropologist*, 104 (3).

— (2006) interview with *Asia Source*: www.asiasource.org/news/special_reports/lila.cfm

Ackerly, A. B. and B. D'Costa (2005) 'Transnational Feminism: Political Strategies and Theoretical Resources', Department of International Relations, Australian National University.

Afghanistan Independent Human Rights Commission (AIHRC) (2006), www.rawa/prg/wom.ihrc.htm

Afghanistan Insurgency Assessment (2005), www.sensilcouncil.net

Afghanland (2005) 'Afghanland culture pashtunwali': www.afghanland.com/culture/pashtunwali.html

Afghan Women's Mission, www.afghanwomensmission.org

Afshar, H. (1989) 'Gender Roles and the "Moral Economy of Kin" among Pakistani Women in West Yorkshire', *New Community*, 15.

— (2005) 'Women's Rights and Islam: Can Things Change?': www.royalphil.arts.gla.ac.uk

— (2006) 'Feminisms, Women and Human Rights: Some Illustrations from Iran', unpublished paper.

Afshar, H., R. Aitkin and M. Franks (2005) 'Feminisms, Islamophobia and Identities', *Political Studies*, 53.

Aftab, O. (2005) 'Bound for the City: A Study of Rural to Urban Labour Migration in Afghanistan', Kabul: AREU (Afghan Research and Evaluation Unit).

Aga Khan Development Network (2004) 'Women's Opium Research, Ishkashim, Zeback and Lower Wakhan', Kabul: Aga Khan Development Network.

Ahmed, L. (1992) *Women and Gender in Islam: Historical Roots of a Modern Debate*, New Haven, CT, and London: Yale University Press.

— (1999) *A Border Passage, from Cairo to America, a Women's Journey*, London: Penguin.

Al-Ali, N. (2003) 'Fundamentalisms and Secularisms in Muslim Societies', in *Women's Teach-in: Antimilitarism, Fundamentalisms/Secularism and Civil Liberties & Anti-Terrorism Legislation after September 11th 2001*, WLUML (Women Living Under Muslim Laws), Occasional Paper No. 14.

Alberts, H. (2003) 'Researching Self-employed Immigrant Women in Hanover', in M. Morokvasic et al. (eds), *Crossing Borders and Shifting Boundaries*, Vol. I: *Gender on the Move*, Opladen: Leske & Budrich.

Ali, T. (2002) *The Clash of Fundamentalisms: Crusades, Jihads, Modernity*, London: Verso.

Amani, W. (2005): www.iwpr.net

Amin, S. (2003) *Obsolescent Capitalism, Contemporary Politics and Global Disorder*, London: Zed Books.

Amnesty International (2003) 'Afghanistan, "No-one listens to us and no-one treats us as human beings": justice denied to women: www.web.amnesty.org/library/index

AREU (Afghan Research and Evaluation Unit) (2005a) 'Afghans in Karachi: Migration, Settlement and Social Networks', Kabul: AREU.

— (2005b) 'Conference on Afghan Population and Movement', Kabul: AREU.

— (2005c) 'Transnational Networks and Migration from Herat to Iran', Kabul: AREU.

— (2006a) 'Conference on Afghan Population Movements', Islamabad, Kabul: AREU.

— (2006b) 'Afghans in Peshawar, Migration, Settlements and Social Networks', Kabul: AREU.

Asian Development Bank (2005) www.adb.org/Documents/Periodicals/ADB_review/2005/vol37-6/opium-economy.asp

Bahramitash, R. (2005) 'The War on Terror, Feminist Orientalism and Orientalist Feminism: Case Studies of Two North American Bestsellers', *Critique: Critical Middle Eastern Studies*, 14 (2).

Barakat, S. (2004) 'Reconstructing War-torn Societies, Afghanistan', *Third World Quarterly* Series, Basingstoke: Palgrave Macmillan.

Barakat, S. and G. Wardell (2001) 'Capitalising on Capacities of Afghan Women: Women's role in Afghanistan's Reconstruction and Development', *InFocus Programme on Crisis*

Response and Reconstruction, International Labour Organization: www.ilo.org/public/english/crisis/index.htm

BBC World Service, www.bbcworldservice.com

Bhatia, M., K. Lanigan and P. Wilkinson (2004) 'Minimal Investments, Minimal Results: The Failure of Security Policy in Afghanistan', Kabul: AREU.

Brodsky, A. E. (2003) *With All Our Strength: The Revolutionary Association of the Women of Afghanistan*, New York and London: Routledge.

Bujis, W. (ed.) (1993) *Migrant Women: Crossing Boundaries and Changing Identities*, Oxford: Berg.

Callinicos, A. (2003) *The New Mandarins of American Power*, London: Polity Press.

— (2006) *The Resources of Critique*, Cambridge: Polity Press.

Christian Aid (2004) 'The Politics of Poverty: Aid in the New Cold War', London: Christian Aid.

CIA (2005) 'Afhanistan', in *Factbook: The World, 2005*: www.cia.gov/publications/factbook/geos/af.html

Cockburn, C. (2003) 'Feminist Antimilitarism', in *Women's Teach-In: Antimilitarism, Fundamentalisms/Secularism and Civil Liberties & Anti-Terrorism Legislation after September 11th 2001*, WLUML (Women Living Under Muslim Laws), Occasional Paper No. 14.

Cursor, www.cursor.org/stories/civilian_death.htm

Duffield, M. (2002) *Global Governance and the New Wars: The Merging of Development and Security*, London: Zed Books.

Dupree, N. H. (1984) 'Revolutionary Rhetoric and Afghan Women in Afghanistan', in N. Shahrani and R. Canfield (eds), *Revolution and Rebellions in Afghanistan, Anthropological Perspectives*, Berkeley: Institute of International Studies, University of California.

— (1998) *The Women of Afghanistan*, Kabul: Swedish Committee for Afghanistan.

Ebadi, S. (2006) *Iran Awakening: A Memoir of Revolution and Hope*, New York: Random House.

Ebrahimi, Z. (2002) 'Moshkele Tabeyate zanan: The Problem of Women's Nationality', *Zanan* (Farsi-language women's journal), Tehran.

— (2004a) 'Ezdevaje zanan ba mardane khareji: The Problem of Women Marrying Foreigners', *Zanan* (Farsi-language women's journal), Tehran.

— (2004b) 'Moshkele ezdevaje zanan ba mardane khareji: The Problem of Women Marrying with Foreign Men', *Zanan* (Farsi-language women's journal), Tehran.

Eisenstein, Z. (2004) *Against Empire: Feminisms, Racism, and the West*, London and New York: Zed Books.

Elshtain, J. B. (1995) *Women and War*, London and Chicago, IL: University of Chicago Press.

Enloe, C. H. (2004) *The Curious*

Feminist: Searching for Women in a New Age of Empire, Berkeley and London: University of California Press.

Erel, U. et al. (2003) 'Skilled Migrant Women and Citizenship', in M. Morokvasic et al. (eds), *Crossing Borders and Shifting Boundaries*, Vol. I: *Gender on the Move*, Opladen: Leske & Budrich.

ESRC (Economic Social Research Council) (2007) *Society Today*: www.esrcsocietytoday.ac.uk

Financial Times (2005–06), www.financialtimes.co.uk/afghanistan

Flanders, L. (2004) *Bushwomen: Tales of a Cynical Species*, London and New York: Verso.

Giles, W. et al. (eds) (1996) *Development and Diaspora: Gender and the Refugee Experience*, Toronto: Artemis Enterprises.

Giustozzi, A. (2003) 'Respectable Warlords? The Politics of State-building in post-Taliban Afghanistan', Working Paper No. 22, Crisis States Programme Development, London: Research Centre, London School of Economics: www.crisisstates.com

— (2004) 'Building Strategies in Afghanistan', Working Paper No. 51, Crisis States Programme Development, London: Research Centre, London School of Economics: www.crisisstates.com

Glatzer, B. (1998) 'Is Afghanistan on the Brink of Ethnic and Tribal Disintegration?', in W. Maley (ed.), *Fundamentalism Reborn? Afghanistan and the Taliban*, London: Hurst and Co.

— (2001) 'War and Boundaries in Afghanistan: Significance and Relativity of Local and Social Boundaries', in *Weld des Islams*, Leiden: Brill.

— (2002) 'The Pashtun Tribal System', in G. Pfeffer and D. K. Behera (eds), *Concepts of Tribal Society*, New Delhi: Concept Publishers.

Guardian (2005–06), www.guardian.co.uk/afghanistan

Haddad, Y. Y. (2006) *Muslim Women in America: The Challenges of Islamic Identity Today*, Oxford: Oxford University Press.

Hagopian, E. C. (2004) *Civil Rights in Peril: The Targeting of Arabs and Muslims*, London: Pluto Press.

Harris, C. (2004) *Control and Subversion: Gender Relations in Tajikistan*, London: Pluto Press.

Harvey, D. (2003) *The New Imperialism*, Oxford: Oxford University Press.

— (2005) *A Brief History of Neoliberalism*, New York: Oxford University Press.

Harzig, C. (2003) 'Immigration Policies: A Gendered Historical Comparison', in M. Morokvasic et al. (eds), *Crossing Borders and Shifting Boundaries*, Vol. I: *Gender on the Move*, Opladen: Leske & Budrich.

Hassan, R. 'Religious Conservatism': www.irfi.org/article_101_150/religious_conservatism.htm

— 'Religious Consultation': www.religiousconsultation.org/hassan.htm

— (2002) 'Muslim Women's Rights: A Contemporary Debate', in S. Mehta (ed.), *Women for Afghan Women: Shattering Myths and Claiming the Future*, Basingstoke: Palgrave Macmillan.

Hoodfar, H. (2004) 'Families on the Move: The Changing Role of Afghan Refugee Women in Iran': www.brill.nl

Human Rights Watch (2001): www.hrw.org/report/2001/afgha3/afgwrd

— (2004) 'Between Hope and Fear: Intimidation and Attacks against Women in Public Life in Afghanistan', Human Rights Watch Briefing Paper, New York.

ILO (International Labour Organization) (2006) *Afghan Households in Iran: Profile and Impact*, Geneva: ILO.

Indra, D. (1989) 'Ethnic Human Rights and Feminist Theory: Gender Implications for Refugee Studies and Practice', *Journal of Refugee Studies*, 2: 221–42.

— (2003) *Engendering Forced Migration: Theory and Practice*, New York and Oxford: Berghahn Books.

Islam, S. and S. Hassan (2004) 'The Wretched of the Nations: The West's Role in Human Rights Violations in the Bangladesh War of Independence', in A. Jones (ed.), *Genocide, War Crimes and the West, History and Complicity*, London and New York: Zed Books.

Johnson, C. and J. Leslie (2004) *Afghanistan: The Mirage of Peace*, London and New York: Zed Books.

Jones, S. (2003) 'A Feminist Antimilitarism', in *Women's Teach-in: Antimilitarism, Fundamentalisms/Secularism and Civil Liberties & Anti-Terrorism Legislation after September 11th 2001*, WLUML (Women Living Under Muslim Laws), Occasional Paper No. 14.

Kandiyoti, D. (2005) *The Politics of Gender and Reconstruction in Afghanistan*, United Nations Research Institute for Social Development (UNRISD), Occasional Paper, Geneva: UNRISD.

Kian-Thiebaut, A. (2005) 'Iran and Afghanistan', in S. Joseph (ed.), *Encyclopaedia of Women and Islamic Cultures*, Vol. 2, *Family, Law and Politics*, Leiden: Brill.

Kirk and Winthrop (2006) 'The Impact of Women Teachers on Girls' Education', UNESCO.

Kerr, J., E. Sprenger and A. Symington (2004) *The Future of Women's Rights: Global Visions and Strategies*, London and New York: Zed Books.

Lenz, I. et al. (eds) (2002) *Crossing Borders and Shifting Boundaries*, Vol II: *Gender, Identities, and Networks*, Opladen: Leske & Budrich.

Long, N. (ed.) (1992) *Battlefields of Knowledge: The Interlocking of Theory and Practice in Social Research and Development*, New York and London: Routledge.

Lutz, H. (2002) 'The Long Shadows of the Past. The New Europe at a Crossroad', in I. Lenz et al. (eds), *Crossing Borders and Shifting Boundaries*, Vol. II: *Gender, Identities, and Networks*, Opladen: Leske & Budrich.

MacDonald, L. (2006) 'Islamic Feminisms, Ideas and Experiences of Convert Women in Britain', unpublished PhD thesis, Centre for Women's Studies, York University.

Makhmalbaf, M. (2001) *Afghan Alphabet*, film, Iran.

Makhmalbaf, S. (2004) *At Five in the Afternoon*, film, Iran.

Matsuoka, A. and J. Sorenson (2003) 'Eritrean Canadian Refugee Households as Sites of Gender Renegotiation', in D. Indra (ed.), *Engendering Forced Migration, Theory and Practice*, New York and Oxford: Berghahn.

Mernissi, F. (1997) *Forgotten Queens of Islam*, Minneapolis: University of Minnesota Press.

— (2001) *Scheherazade Goes West: Different Cultures, Different Harems*, New York: Washington Square Press.

— (2002) *Islam and Democracy: Fear of the Modern World*, Cambridge, MA: Perseus.

Meshkini, M. (2005) *Stray Dog*, film, Iran.

Mir-Hosseini, Z. (2002) 'Religious Modernists and the Woman's Question: Challenges and Complicities', in E. Hooglund (ed.), *Iran in Transition*, Syracuse, NY: Syracuse University Press.

— (2003) 'The Construction of Gender in Islamic Legal Thought and Strategies for Reform', paper presented to the Sisters in Islam Regional Workshop, Islamic Family Law and Justice for Muslim Women, 8–10 June 2001: www.brill.nl

Mir-Hosseini, Z. and R. Tapper (2006) *Islam and Democracy in Iran: Eshkevari and the Quest for Reform*, London: I.B. Tauris.

Mohanty, C. T. et al. (eds) (1991) *Third World Women and the Politics of Feminism*, Bloomington: Indiana University Press.

Momsen, J. and V. Kinnaird (eds) (1993) *Different Places, Different Voices: Gender and Development in Africa, Asia and Latin America*, London and New York: Routledge.

Monsutti, A. (2004) 'Cooperation, Remittances, and Kinship among the Hazaras', *Iranian Studies*, 37 (2).

— (2005) *War and Migration: Social Networks and Economic Strategies of the Hazaras of Afghanistan*, New York and London: Routledge.

Morokvasic, M., U. Erel and K. Shinozaki (eds) (2003) *Crossing Borders and Shifting Boundaries*, Vol. I: *Gender on the Move*, Opladen: Leske & Budrich.

Moser, C. and F. Clark (eds) (2001) *Victims, Perpetrators or Actors? Gender, Armed Conflict and Political Violence*, London and New York: Zed Books.

Narayan, U. (1997) *Disclosing Cultures: Identities, Traditions and Third World Feminism*, London: Routledge.

Nawa, F. (2002) 'Two Identities, One Mission', in S. Mehta (ed.), *Women for Afghan Women: Shattering Myths and Claiming the Future*, New York and Basingstoke: Palgrave Macmillan.

— (2005) www.corpwatch.org

Orlando, V. (1999) *Nomadic Voices of Exile: Feminine Identity in Francophone Literature of the Maghreb*, Athens: Ohio University Press.

Pain, A. (2004) 'The Impact of the Opium Poppy Economy on Household Livelihoods: Evidence from the Wakhan Corridor and Khustak Valley in Badakhshan', Kabul: Aga Khan Development Network.

Pain, A. and J. Goodhand (2002) 'Afghanistan: Current Employment and Socio-economic Situation and Prospects', *InFocus Programme on Crisis Response and Reconstruction*, International Labour Organization: www.ilo.org/public/english/crisis/index.htm

Pajhwok Afghan News (2006) 23 October: www.rawa.org/bamyan_cave.htm

Parpart, J. and M. Marchand (eds) (1995) 'Exploding the Canon: An Introduction/Conclusion', in *Feminism/Postmodernism/Development*, London and New York: Routledge.

Phizacklea, A. (2003) 'Transnationalism, Gender and Global Workers', in M. Morokvasic et al. (eds), *Crossing Borders and Shifting Boundaries*, Vol. I: *Gender on the Move*, Opladen: Leske & Budrich.

Phoenix, A. (1998) 'Dealing with Difference, the Recursive and the New', *Ethnic and Racial Studies*, 21.

Portes, A. (1997) 'Immigration Theory for a New Century: Some Problems and Opportunities', *International Migration Review*, 31.

Poya, M. (E. Rostami-Povey) (1999) *Women, Work and Islamism: Ideology and Resistance in Iran*, London: Zed Books.

Rajaee, B. (2000) 'The Politics of Refugee Policy in Post-revolutionary Iran', *Middle East Journal*, 54.

Rashid, A. (2000) *Taliban, Islam, Oil and the New Great Game in Central Asia*, London: I.B. Tauris.

— (2001) *Taliban, Militant Islam, Oil and Fundamentalism in Central Asia*, New Haven, CT: Yale University Press.

— (2006) 'How to Help Afghanistan: A Global Response to the Crisis', *Washington Post*: www.washingtonpost.com

RAWA (The Revolutionary Association of the Women of Afghanistan), www.rawa.org

Rees, J. (2006) *Imperialism and Resistance*, London: Routledge.

Rostami-Povey, E. (2001) 'Feminist Contestations of Institutional Domains in Iran', *Feminist Review Collective*, 69, London: Routledge.

— (2004a) 'Women in Afghanistan, Passive Victims of the Borqa or Active Social Participants?', in H. Afshar (ed.), *Development, Women, and War: Feminist Perspectives, A Development in Practice Reader*, Oxford: Oxfam.

— (2004b) 'Civil Society in Afghanistan', in S. Joseph (ed.), *Encyclopaedia of Women and Islamic Cultures*, Vol. 2: *Family, Law and Politics*, Leiden: Brill Academic.

— (2004c), 'Political–Social Movements. Unions and Workers' Movements in Iran', in S. Joseph (ed.), *Encyclopaedia of Women and Islamic Cultures*, Vol. 2: *Family, Law and Politics*, Leiden: Brill Academic.

— (2004d) 'Trade Unions and Women's NGOs in Iran', *Development in Practice*, 14 (1&2), Oxford: Oxfam.

— (2005) 'Trade Unions and Women's NGOs, Diverse Civil Society Organisations in Iran', in D. Eade and A. Leather (eds), *Development NGOs and Labour Unions: Terms of Engagement*, Bloomfield, CT: Kumarian Press.

— (2007a) 'Gender, Agency and Identity, the Case of Afghan Women in Afghanistan, Pakistan and Iran', in H. Afshar (ed.), Special Section on Islam and Female Identity in the Middle East, *Journal of Development Studies*, 43 (2), London: Routledge, Taylor and Francis.

— (2007b) 'Afghan Refugees in Iran, Pakistan, the U.K. and the US and Life after Return: A Comparative Gender Analysis', in D. Tober (ed.), Special Issue: Afghan Refugees, *Iranian Studies*, 40 (2), London: Routledge, Taylor and Francis.

Rubin, B. (1995) *The Fragmentation of Afghanistan. State Formation and Collapse in the International System*, New Haven, CT, and London: Yale University Press.

— (1997) 'Women and Pipelines: Afghanistan's Proxy Wars', *International Affairs*, 73 (2).

— (2002) *The Fragmentation of Afghanistan*, New Haven, CT: Yale University Press.

Rundle, C. (2004) *From Colwyn Bay to Kabul*, Durham: Memoir Club.

Sadr, S. (2002) 'Tou digar Irani nisty va bayad beravi: You are No Longer Iranian and You Have to Go', *Zanan* (Farsi-language women's journal), Tehran.

Said, E. W. (1979) *Orientalism*, New York: Vintage.

— (1993) *Culture and Imperialism*, London: Chatto and Windus.

— (1996) *Representations of the Intellectual*, New York: Vintage.

Schutte, S. (2004) 'Urban Vulnerability in Afghanistan: Case Studies from Three Cities', Kabul: AREU.

Scott, J. (1990) *Domination and the Arts of Resistance: Hidden Transcripts*, New Haven, CT: Yale University Press.

Security and Development Policy Group, www.senliscouncil.net

Sedra, M. (2002) 'Challenging the Warlord Culture Security Sector Reform in Post-Taliban Afghanistan', Bonn International Center for Conversion: www.bicc.de

Shah, S. (2000). *Where Do I Belong?*, London.

Shahrani, N. (1984) 'Introduction: Marxist "Revolution" and Islamic Resistance in Afghanistan', in N. Shahrani and R. L. Canfield (eds), *Revolutions and Rebellions in Afghanistan, Anthropological Perspectives*, Berkeley: Institute of International Studies, University of California Press.

Simonsen, S. G. (2004) 'Ethnicising Afghanistan? Inclusion and Exclusion in post-Bonn Institution Building', *Third World Quarterly*, 25.

South Asia Media, www.southasiamedia.net

Stanley, L. and S. Wise (2000) 'But the Empress Has No Clothes! Some Awkward Questions about the "Missing Revolution" in Feminist Theory', *Feminist Theory*, 1, London: Sage.

Steel, J. (2006), *Guardian*, 20 October.

Stewart, P. and A. Strathern (eds) (2000) *Identity Work, Constructing Pacific Lives*, Pittsburgh, PA: University of Pittsburgh Press.

Stiglitz, J. (2006) *Making Globalisation Work*, London: Allen Lane.

Suhrke, A. (2006) *The Limits of State Building: The Role of International Assistance in Afghanistan*, Bergen: Chr. Michelsen Institute.

Sultan, M. (2002) 'Hope in Afghanistan', in S. Mehta (ed.), *Women for Afghan Women: Shattering Myths and Claiming the Future*, New York and Basingstoke: Palgrave Macmillan.

Tapper, N. (1984) 'Causes and Consequences of the Abolition of Bride Price in Afghanistan', in N. Shahrani and R. L. Canfield (eds), *Revolution and Rebellions in Afghanistan, Anthropological Perspectives*, Berkeley: Institute of International Studies, University of California.

Tickner, J. A. (2001) *Gendering World Politics: Issues and Approaches in the Post-Cold War Era*, New York: Columbia University Press.

Turner, B. S. (1993) *Citizenship and Social Theory*, London: Sage.

UNDP (United Nations Development Programme) (2005) 'Afghanistan's Future Holds Promise and Peril'.

UNHCR (UN High Commissioner for Refugees) (2003 and 2004) *Statistical Yearbook*.

UNICEF (2006), www.rawa.org/UNICEF.htm.

UN, IRIN (2006) 'Bitter-sweet Harvest: Afghanistan's New War', IRIN web special, 'The Threat of Opium to Afghanistan and the Region', *IRIN News*: www.irinnews.org

UNODC (UN Office on Drugs and Crime) (2004) 'Afghanistan Opium Survey 2004': www.undoc.org/af/en/report_surveys.html

— (2006) 'UN Drugs Chief Sounds Warning about Afghan Opium Production, Cocaine Consumption in Europe': www.unodc.org

UNSC (UN Security Council) (2001) Resolution 1368, 12 September 2001; and Resolution 1373, 28 September 2001.

USA Today (2006) 16 November: www.usatoday.com

Vertovec, S. (1999) 'Conceiving and Researching Transnationalism', *Ethnic and Racial Studies*, 22.

Viner, K. (2002), 'Feminism as Imperialism', *Guardian*, 21 September 2002.

Vorgetts, F. (2002) 'A Vision of Justice, Equality and Peace', in S. Mehta (ed.), *Women for Afghan Women: Shattering Myths and Claiming the Future*, New York and Basingstoke: Palgrave Macmillan.

Wood, E. M. (2003) *Empire of Capital*, London and New York: Verso.

World Bank (2004) 'Afghanistan: State Building, Sustaining Growth, and Reducing Poverty', Washington, DC: World Bank.

— (2006) 'Afghanistan, Pervasive Gender Gaps in Afghanistan Need Urgent Addressing': www.worldbanki.org.af

Young, I. M. (2003) 'The Logic of Masculinist Protection: Reflections on the Current Security State', *Signs: Journal of Women in Culture and Society*, 29.

Yusuf Daoud. Z. (2002) 'Miss Afghanistan: A Story of a Nation', in S. Mehta (ed.), *Women for Afghan Women: Shattering Myths and Claiming the Future*, New York and Basingstoke: Palgrave Macmillan.

Index

11 September 2001 attacks, 1, 20, 22, 45; effects on Afghan women, 111–26
7 June attacks, effects on Afghan women, 111–26

abduction of children, 46
Abdulsatar, from Los Angeles, 116–17
Abdur Rahman Khan, 9
Abu-Lughod, Lila, 140
addiction to drugs, 56–6, 75
Adela, from Peshawar, 95
Afghan Women Lawyers and Professional Association, 34
Afghan Women's Council (AWC), 31, 53
Afghan Women's Network (AWN), 53, 107
Afghan Women newspaper, 32
Afghanistan: assessment of quality of life in, 74–8; establishment of borders of, 9; nation-state building in, 14; natural resources of, 67; population of, 80
Afghanistan Independent Human Rights Commission (AIHRC), 1
Afghanistan Insurgency Assessment, 49
Afghanistan Research and Evaluation Unit, 81
Afshar, Haleh, 135
Aga Khan Development Network, 56
agency, 3–9
agriculture, 56; women in, 17, 84
Ahmed, an engineer, 67
Ahmed, Leila, 135; *Women and Gender in Islam*, 138
aid community, as surrogate state, 21
airlines, private, 54
Aisha, wife of Muhammad, 135
Alama, from Los Angeles, 113
Amanullah Khan, 10
al-Amr bi-al-ma.ruf wa-al-nahy an almunkar, 24
Ashraf, Orzala, 33
Aymal, from Los Angeles, 125

Balkhi, Rabia, 16
Balkhi, Saddiqa, 31
Bamiyan, University of, 33–4
Barakzai, Shukria, 64
Bas Gul, a teacher in Peshawar, 102
beard and hair, growing of, 30
begging by women, 19, 28, 32, 47, 64, 69, 74, 85
Bin Laden, Osama, 22, 41
Blair, Tony, 45, 123, 124
Bollywood culture, 70–4
bombing of Afghanistan, 1, 2, 40–1, 70, 115
bonded labour, 57, 86
Bonyade Zaynab Kobra organization, 87
British empire, 9
Brzezinski, Zbigniew, 20
burqa, 6–7, 36, 37, 49, 76
Bush, George W., 40–1, 44, 45, 63, 123, 124

carpet weaving, 17–18, 21, 29, 47, 58, 85
Carter, Jimmy, 20
chaddari, 6–7, 11, 18, 21, 26–7, 36, 37, 75, 116, 123, 133
cheap labour, Afghans as, 85

children: suffering of, 25–6; child labour, 1, 19; child mortality, 41
civil war period, 19–26
cluster bombs, use of, 40
code of honour *see* honour codes
condoms, distribution of, 110
Convention on the Elimination of All Discrimination Against Women (CEDAW), 60, 63
corruption, 42, 50, 73
crime, 75
currency, valueless, 49

Daoud, Mohammed, 10
Daoud, Zohra Yusuf, 1
Dari language, 3, 5, 68, 73, 88, 96, 98, 102, 120
death sentence, for women, 62
debt, 57, 86
democracy, 64, 129; US model of, 44–5
Department for International Development (DFID), 97
diasporic consciousness, 94–8
disarmament of armed groups, 64
division of labour, 85; traditional, 58
divorce, 106; non-registration of, 62
doctors, 52; women as, 30
dress and dress codes, 24, 76, 103, 111–12; American, 122; Islamic, 37
Durand, Mortimer, 9
Durand Line, 9

education, 65–6; at heart of women's struggles, 33; enrolment figures, 65; in exile, 101–2, 111–12; informal, 66; of women, 12, 13, 35, 60–1, 83, 103–4, 125; schooling, costs of, 109; secret schools, 32, 33, 34, 36, 37; Taliban closure of schools, 25; women's right to, 29, 31 *see also* girls, education of
elections, 55, 63–4
electricity, supply of, 46, 58, 70
Elham, from London, 90–1
empowerment of women, 29
English language, 98, 120
ethnicity, 3–9
exile, and identity, 80–128

family: erosion of, 19; extended, 119–20
family law, 133; reform of, 11
family relations, 102–11
Farida, from Pakistan, 106
Farsi language, 3, 68, 96, 98, 102
Fatana, from Pakistan, 99, 100
Fatemeh, a teacher, 86–7
female-headed households, 27, 31, 58, 92, 108
feminism, 135; among Afghan women, 139; and Islam, 141; diversity of, 141; rejected in Afghanistan, 142; Western, 140, 141
Feminist Majority Foundation, 123, 141
Feriba, from Mazar-e-Sharif, 47–8
Feze, a returnee, 60–1
Fouzia, a returnee, 51

Gailani, Fatima, 16
gender, use of term, 51
gender equality, rhetoric of, 138
gender mainstreaming, 138
gender relations, 1–3, 3–9, 17–19, 55, 59, 77, 92–3, 134; historically specific, 8, 9; in Islamic context, 102–11; not static, 18
gender segregation, 18, 106
Geneva Convention, 47
Ghamam, member of Vocational Training Centre, 30
girls: education of, 1, 23, 86–8, 91 (not sent to school, 66); sale of, 60

Habibeh, a teacher in Tehran, 102
Hajara, an NGO activist, 72

Halima, a rights activist, 49
Halimeh, from Khorasan, 105
Hamasa, from Jalalabad, 129
Hami organization, 107
handicrafts activity of women, 30, 32, 58, 84
Hanifa, from Pakistan, 95
Harvey, David, 44
Hassan, Riffat, 135
Hazaras, 5, 80, 82, 94–5, 98–100; massacre of, 6
Hazaragi dialect, 5
Hekmatyar, Gulbuddin, 43
heroin trade, 49
hijab, 116, 119, 122, 137; and Muslim identity, 113
HIV/AIDS, 110
Homaira, a returnee, 71
honour codes, 4, 18, 60, 61
honour killings, 72, 133
Hoquqmal, Mahbuba, 31, 59, 62–3
housing, right to, 53
Human Rights Watch, 55
Humanitarian Assistance for the Women and Children of Afghanistan (HAWCA), 33, 53, 86, 88

identification cards, 76
identity, 3–9, 80–128; communal, 17–19 (not absolute, 18); cultural, 68–9; of women, fluid, 3
illiteracy *see* literacy and illiteracy
imperial agenda, challenging of, 139
imperial domination, challenge to, 14
Inayatollah, from Mazar-e-Sharif, 65
individuality, 93; western culture of, 51
internally displaced people, 20–1, 27, 40
International Security Assistance Force (ISAF), 2, 42, 45, 46, 49, 130, 131
Internet, 51, 70, 71, 72
Iran, 7, 8, 14, 68–9, 134; Afghans living in, 80, 137; diasporic consciousness in, 94–8; migration to, 80–9; women's rights in, 63
Iranian Adult Literacy Organization, 97
Iranian NGO Training Centre (INGOTC), 107
Iraqification, 42
Iraqis, solidarity with, 114, 121
Islam, 4, 12, 22, 93, 130, 132, 134–5; and gender relations, 102–11; attacks on, 134; collective identity of, 99; hostility to, 90; rights of women in, 51; status of women in, 24, 136, 139; used to justify war, 8
Islamic Centre for Political and Cultural of Afghan Women, 31
Islamophobia, 91, 114–15; in London, 112; resistance to, 122
Ismailis, 5

Johnson, Chris, 43

Kabul, University of, 33; closure of, 25
Kamal, Meena Keshwar, 17
Kandiyoti, Deniz, 60
Khadija, wife of Muhammad, 135
Khalg faction, 10

land, rights over, 58
land reform, 10
Leslie, Jolyon, 43
life expectancy, 41
literacy and illiteracy, 25, 34–5, 41, 53, 66, 88; programmes, 12
Loya Jirga, women's participation in, 59, 107

Madarese Khodgardan, 86, 101, 107
Madrassa system, 23, 25, 88; provides recruiting centres, 43

mahram, 6–7, 11, 18, 36, 108; hiring of, 36–7
Mahtab, from Iran, 83–4
Malalai, a teacher, 86
Malalai, from Los Angeles, 122
Malalai, Pashtun heroine, 4
Malileh, from Iran, 100
malnutrition, 25, 27
Mansoora, a teacher, 65
Mansoora, an NGO activist, 74
marriage, 49–50, 71, 106, 133, 135; age of, 105; arranged, 91; forced, 22, 29, 61; intermarriage, 82, 90; non-registration of, 62; under-age, 66; women's refusal of, 60, 105
Marzieh, from Iran, 82–3
masculinist protection of women, 124
Massouda, a returnee, 73
Massuda, from Peshawar, 107–8
matrilineality, 4
Mayward, Battle of, 4
Mazar-e-Sharif, bombing of, 40
men: diverse attitudes of, 130; experience of subordination, 37; male domination, 7, 14; opposed to domination, 7; respect for women, 106, 109; role of, 92–3 (in family, 108–9) *see also mahram*
menstruation, 27
Mernissi, Fatema, 135
middle class, 80, 82, 89
migration, 19, 54; rural-to-urban, 46, 69–70, 75 *see also* internal displacement
Mir-Hosseini, Ziba, 136
Mirwaiz, from Mazar-e-Sharif, 47
mobile phones, 71, 72
Mohammad, a journalist, 74–5
Muhammad, Prophet, 35
Mujaheddin, 11, 21, 22, 29, 81, 122; US funding of, 20

Nadia, a journalist, 86
Nadir Shah, 10
Nahid, an NGO worker, 107
Najia, from Jalalabad, 51
Najia, from London, 121
Najia, from Los Angeles, 91
Nargis, a returnee, 51
Nasira, member of Afghan Women Council, 32–3
Nastaran, from London, 111
National Union of Women of Afghanistan, 27
Nehzate Savadamozi movement, 86
neo-conservatism, 45
non-governmental organizations (NGOs), 14, 34, 35, 42, 45, 46, 47, 48, 49, 50–1, 52, 59, 138; employment of Afghan women, 50, 67; women's organizations, 103, 133 (workers killed, 2)
North Atlantic Treaty Organization (NATO), 2, 45

Omar Koshy, tradition of, 100
opium: anti-drug campaign, 56; area of cultivation, 56; children's use of, 57; production of, 21
opium economy, 13, 42, 49, 50, 55–9, 75; women's participation in, 58
orphanages, 88–9

Paikan, Suraya, 34
Pakistan, 7, 9, 14, 20, 41, 68–9, 134; Afghans living in, 80; diasporic consciousness in, 94–8; migration to, 80–9
Pakistanization of Southern Afghanistan, 49
Palestinians, solidarity with, 114, 121
Parcham faction, 10
Parliament, women in, 2, 34
Parlyka, Suraya, 27, 29
Parvana, a university student, 21

Pashto language, 4, 88, 96, 98
Pashto Belt, 49
Pashtuns, 4–5, 9, 10, 35, 80, 82, 94, 98–100, 105; in government, 55; treatment of women, 23
Pashtunwali, 4, 5, 23
patriarchy, 7, 8, 103, 107, 117, 129, 130, 133, 135; challenges to, 37
Payam-e Zan, 16
People's Democratic Party of Afghanistan (PDPA), 10
pornography, 70–4
poverty, 32, 42, 46, 52, 53, 57, 58, 63, 70, 75
prayer, 36, 65, 119
pregnancy, 57
prisoners, women, freeing of, 64
private companies, foreign, 53–5
privatization, 21, 44, 54
professional women, 28
Provisional Reconstruction Teams (PRTs), 47–8

al-Qaida, 2, 20, 22, 40, 41, 43, 75–6
Qur'an, 12, 13, 104

Rabi, Humera, 34
Rabia Balkhi Women's Hospital, 30
racism, 112, 114, 133; experienced by Afghans in exile, 83–4, 89–90, 91, 95, 97, 98
Rahima, Dr, 30
Rahima, from London, 118–19
Rahima, from Los Angeles, 114
rape, 13, 21, 26, 29, 49, 53, 74, 113; in jail, 62
Rasoola, an NGO activist, 67
Ratib, Anahita, 16
refugees, 27, 81; return of, 67–70
Revolutionary Association of the Women of Afghanistan (RAWA), 16–17, 53, 88
Rice, Condoleezza, 140
rights of women, 10, 14, 31, 43, 53, 60, 117, 129, 135, 137; depoliticized, 138; in Iran, 63; in Islam, 51; rhetoric of, used to justify war, 40, 123–4, 142; to own property, 58; Western models of, 12
road building, 41
Rogya, a returnee, 69
Ruhullah, murdered in London, 112
Russia, 9

Saffiullah, from Los Angeles, 121
Said, Edward, 97–8
Sakina, an NGO worker, 100
Sakkineh, a campaign worker, 110
Saleha, from Peshawar, 83
Saleha, from London, 111
Salima, an NGO worker, 107
Samar, Sima, 59
Sarabi, Habiba, 59
sargardan (wanderers), 121
Satar, Abdul, 74
Saudi Arabia, 20
'saving women', 124, 138–9, 140
Scheffer, Jaap de Hoop, 42–3
schools, self-run, 86–8 *see* also education, secret schools
secret organizations of women, 13
'security and development', 50
Seddiqi, Suhaila, 59
segregation *see* gender segregation
self-burning of women, 1, 61–2, 123
Setara, from London, 119
sex segregation, 10
sex workers, women as, 1, 19, 26, 28, 32, 47, 64, 70, 74
Shafia, an activist, 64
Shafiqa, director of Vocational Training Centre, 30
Shah, Shahbibi, 52, 112
Shahida, a returnee, 73
Shahla, a businesswoman, 67
Shahrani, Nazif, 11
Shari'a law, 24, 58, 136; enforcement of, 23

Sherifa, a returnee, 68
Sherkatgah organization, 107
Shi'a community, 5, 22, 80, 82, 83, 85, 98, 100–1
Sima, an activist, 63–4
Smeal, Eleanor, 123
Somayeh, an Iranian volunteer, 25
Soraya, a returnee, 68
state, 53–5; collapse of, 21, 62
students, strike of, 66
Suhail, a journalist, 28
Suhaila, from Los Angeles, 89, 116, 121
suicide, of women, 2, 28, 29 *see also* self-burning of women
suicide bombings, 42
Sunni community, 4, 5, 80, 82, 83, 98, 100–1, 102
Suraya, from Iran, 96

Tahera, from Los Angeles, 114
Tajbanoo, from Los Angeles, 116
Tajiks, 82, 98–100, 102
Taliban, 2, 3, 6, 13, 19–26, 48, 74, 81, 108, 123, 131; fall of, 1, 5; gender policy of, 24; intelligence agency of, 35; resistance and struggle under, 16–39; women under, 26–38
Tapper, Nancy, 11
teachers: pay of, 87; shortages of, 65; women as, 25, 33
television, 50, 70
transnational corporations (TNCs), 44, 54

Union of Soviet Socialist Republics (USSR), 10, 11, 38; collapse of, 20; expenditure on Afghanistan, 19–20; invasion of Afghanistan, 11, 80, 83, 84, 100, 134
United Kingdom (UK), 40, 134; Afghans living in, 14, 80, 111–26; migration to, 89–94; military spending of, 43
United Nations (UN), 48, 49, 50–1, 52, 59, 138; aid provided by, 34; investment in elections, 55; reduces aid to Afghanistan, 25
UN Development Programme (UNDP), 41
UN High Commissioner for Refugees (UNHCR), 31, 42, 81; training of Aghan women, 84
UN Security Council, 45
UN Children's Fund (UNICEF), 1, 86, 88, 97
United States of America (USA), 10, 22, 38, 45, 130, 131, 132, 134; Afghans living in, 14, 80, 111–26; expenditure on Afghanistan, 20; investment in elections, 55; migration to, 89–94; military spending of, 43; National Security Strategy (NSS), 44; policy interests of, 81
universities, women in, 21–2, 26, 137
urbanization, 69
Urdu language, 96, 98
Uzbeks, 5, 82, 98–100; massacre of, 6

veil, voluntary removal of, 10, 12
violence against women, 12, 70, 131
virginity, importance of, 118
virginity test, 61, 72

Wali, Sima, 38, 59
war on terror, 43
warlords, 13, 53–5, 99, 131; in government, 59; relation to opium economy, 55–6
water, supply of, 58
women: as bearers of cultural identity, 92; contribution to economy, 17–18; cooperation among, 6; liberation of, 129, 141; marginalization of, 97, 103; men's respect for, 106; murder

of, 26; pregnancy-related deaths of, 60; respected in community, 17; role in reconstruction, 76–7; secret organizations of, 32; solidarity of, 13; status in Islam, 136, 139; survival strategies of, 28–38; under the Taliban, 26–38; unemployment of, 46, 75; work of, 40, 47–8, 50, 67–9, 108–9 *see also* rights of women; universities, women in *and* work of women
Women's Association of Afghanistan, 30
women's movement, 103–4; in Iran, 137
Women's Vocational Training Centre, 29–30
World Bank, 41, 45, 65
World Trade Organization (WTO), 45

Young, Iris, 124
Yusuf Daoud, Zohra yes, 12

Zahir Shah, 10
Zainab, from London, 93
Zala, from Mazar-e-Sharif, 65
Zanane bee Sarparast organization, 27
Zaynab, from Peshawar, 95
Zubair, from Pakistan, 98

IRAQI WOMEN

Untold Stories From 1948 to the Present

Nadje Sadig Al-Ali

'Al-Ali draws a vivid picture of Iraqi society and politics using intense personal narratives, and offers alternative visions of modern Iraqi history. An absorbing read.' - *Sami Zubaida, Emeritus Professor, Birkbeck, University of London*

'A powerful interrogation of the complex relationships between experience, memory and truth, told through the dynamic narratives of Iraqi women ... a compelling critique of contemporary histories of Iraq which project back into the past relatively newly installed notions of religion and ethnicity.' - *Suad Joseph, Professor of Anthropology & Women's Studies, University of California, Davis*

'A finely nuanced account of the experiences of women in Iraq ... Al-Ali's experience of Iraqi society as an insider/outsider, and her understanding of the political background of her informants, enables her to explore the relationship between experiences, memory and truth in ways which will intrigue and excite her readers.' - *Peter Sluglett, Professor of Middle Eastern History, University of Utah, Salt Lake City*

'[A collection of] the thoughts, memories and experiences of more than 100 women who, at one time or another, have joined Iraq's huge diaspora in America, Britain and Jordan....the pattern [Al-Ali] draws of the way that educated women's lives have changed and rechanged since Iraq's 1958 revolution is fascinating.' - *The Economist*

'A vital and original contribution to the literature on Iraq's modern history and to the literature on gender and women's studies. But at the same time its rich, fascinating and revealing text is enormously readable and accessible' - *Al-Hayat*

Hb ISBN 978 1 84277 744 2
Pb ISBN 978 1 84277 745 9

SEXUAL DECOYS

Gender, Race and War in Imperial Democracy

Zillah Eisenstein

'For Zillah Eisenstein politics is like the air we breathe and the ideas we live - always deserving our deepest attention. In *Sexual Decoys* once again, Eisenstein brilliantly draws us into the profoundly complex gendered politics of war, mobilizing startling constructs like sexual decoys, patriarchal imperialism, neoliberal feminism, and racialized fascist democracy to sharpen our analytic feminist lenses and demystify war cultures. A smart, challenging book for everyone concerned with what it means to live ethically and accountably in the USA of the present.' - *Chandra Talpade Mohanty, Professor of Women's Studies, Syracuse University*

'Zillah Eisenstein's *Sexual Decoys* is an incisive critique of the rightwing mobilization of gender and race for imperial designs. The book insightfully illuminates the contradictions of war waged in the name of spreading democracy. Asking whether terrorism is the new version of the old communist menace, Eisenstein contextualizes current militarization policies, and boldly exposes their noxious fallout for democracy.' - *Ella Shohat, New York University*

'Zillah Eisenstein's latest feminist text is a provocative, insightful reading of the gendered and racialized complexities of the wars in Afganistan and Iraq and the ways in which the metaphor of "sexual and racial decoys" can be deployed to illuminate contemporary US government machinations here and around the globe. Very little escapes Eisenstein's critical gaze: the Bush administration, Laura Bush, Condi Rice, Hillary Clinton, Katrina, Abu Ghraib, Guantanamo, neoliberal/imperial feminism, diversity in the academy. *Sexual Decoys* is sure to be controversial because of its biting critiques of both conservatives and liberals.' - *Beverly Guy-Sheftall, Director of the Women's Research & Resource Center at Spelman College*

Hb ISBN 978 1 84277 816 6
Pb ISBN 978 1 84277 817 3

FROM WHERE WE STAND

War, Women's Activism and Feminist Analysis

Cynthia Cockburn

'Cynthia Cockburn is one of the most valuable and innovative thinkers/ activists/writers helping us all to make sense of women's myriad forms of resistance to war and militarism. She shows how it is they who are crafting fresh thinking about how nationalism, masculinity, imperialism, racism, classism and misogyny each and together fuel militarism and its deadly outcomes. This is a book to open our eyes and move us to action.' - *Cynthia Enloe*

'Cynthia Cockburn is one of the best gender researchers in the world. In this very important book she opens global perspectives on women's politics and the struggle for peace, linking activist experience with up-to-date gender analysis.' - *Raewyn Connell, University of Sydney*

This original study examines women's activism against war in areas as far apart as Sierra Leone, India, Colombia and Palestine. It shows women on different sides of conflicts in the former Yugoslavia and Israel addressing racism and refusing enmity and describes international networks of women opposing US and Western European militarism and the so-called 'war on terror'. These movements, though diverse, are generating an antimilitarist feminism that challenges how war and militarism are understood, both in academic studies and the mainstream anti-war movement. Gender, particularly the form taken by masculinity in a violent sex/gender system, is inseparably linked to economic and ethno-national factors in the perpetuation of war.

Hb ISBN 978 1 84277 550 9
Pb ISBN 978 1 84277 820 3

THE HIDDEN FACE OF EVE

Women in the Arab World

Nawal El Saadawi

with a new foreward by Ronak Husni

'A harrowing expose of the abuse of women in the Arab world' - *London Review of Books*

'Nawal El Saadawi has become something of a heroine for many young Arab women ... a cry from the heart' - *MESA Bulletin*

'The Arab world's leading feminist and iconoclast' - *Fedwa Malti-Davis*

'The leading spokeswoman on the status of women in the Arab world' - *The Guardian*

This powerful account of the oppression of women in the Muslim world remains as shocking today as when it was first published, more than a quarter of a century ago.

Nawal El Saadawi writes out of a powerful sense of the violence and injustice which permeated her society. Her experiences working as a doctor in villages around Egypt, witnessing prostitution, honour killings and sexual abuse, including female circumcision, drove her to give voice to this suffering. She goes on explore the causes of the situation through a discussion of the historical role of Arab women in religion and literature. Saadawi argues that the veil, polygamy and legal inequality are incompatible with the essence of Islam or any human faith.

This edition, complete with a new foreword, lays claim to *The Hidden Face of Eve*'s status as a classic of modern Arab writing.

Hb ISBN 978 1 84277 875 3

Pb ISBN 978 1 84277 874 6

Zed Books
7 Cynthia Street
London N1 9JF
Tel: 020 7837 4014
Fax: 020 7833 3960
www.zedbooks.co.uk